Collection Highlights from the
Memphis Brooks Museum of Art

Collection Highlights from the
Memphis Brooks Museum of Art

Copyright © 2004 by the Board of Directors, Memphis Brooks Museum of Art, Inc. All rights reserved.
Published by the Memphis Brooks Museum of Art, Inc.
Concept Design: Heather Klein and Claudia Towell
Design Layout: Heather Klein
Design Intern: Jaime Borum
Edited: Kaywin Feldman and Marina Pacini
Printed and bound by Starr-Toof, Memphis, Tennessee, United States.

Library of Congress Control Number: 2004111915
ISBN 0-915525-09-7

Memphis Brooks Museum of Art
1934 Poplar Avenue
Overton Park
Memphis, Tennessee 38104
901.544.6200
www.brooksmuseum.org

Cover:
Winslow Homer, American, 1836-1910
Reading by the Brook, det., 1879
Oil on canvas
15 7/8" x 22 3/4" (40.3 cm x 57.8 cm)
Memphis Park Commission Purchase 43.22

Title page and section title pages:
Bamileke
Africa, Cameroon
Elephant Society Mask, det., late 19th century
Raffia, beads, canvas
62 3/4" x 18 1/2" x 8 1/4" (159.4 cm x 47 cm x 21 cm)
Gift of the Director's Council 97.2.1

Roelof Koets
Dutch, 1592-1655
Still Life on a Draped Table, det., ca. 1635
Oil on panel
29 5/8" x 43" (75.2 cm x 109.2 cm)
Memphis Brooks Museum of Art Purchase;
Morrie A. Moss Acquisition Fund 2002.2

Childe Hassam
American, 1859-1935
Apple Blossoms, det., ca. 1885
Oil on wood panel
13 3/8" x 15 1/4" (33.8 cm x 38.8 cm)
Gift of Walter M. Rentschler 67.1

Nam June Paik
South Korean, b. 1932
Vide-O-belisk, det., 2002
Vintage television cabinets, neon elements, and video
232" x 82 1/2" x 84 1/2" (589.3 cm x 209.6 cm x 214.6 cm)
Commissioned by the Memphis Brooks Museum of Art; funds provided by the Morrie A. Moss Acquisition Fund, the Hohenberg Foundation, Wil and Sally Hergenrader, and the Bodine Company 2002.4

This book is dedicated with love and appreciation
to Virginia Clark and Renée Guibao

Catalogue Authors

Walter Robert Brown
Adjunct Curator of Decorative Arts

Kathy Hensley Dumlao
Assistant Curator of Education

Kaywin Feldman
Director

Karleen Vincent Gardner
Associate Curator of Education

Marilyn Masler
Associate Registrar

Marina Pacini
Chief Curator

Ana Vejzovic
Assistant Curator

John Weeden
Exhibitions Manager

Contents

Preface

It has been twenty years since the Memphis Brooks Museum of Art published the last collection catalogue, *Painting and Sculpture Collection: Memphis Brooks Museum of Art*. Completed under the leadership of Douglas Hyland, this book continues to be a vital source of information about the collection, however scarce copies have become. The hardest task of *Collection Highlights from the Memphis Brooks Museum of Art* was the selection of works to be included, since the book is not comprehensive. The authors worked together as a committee to compile the final list of collection highlights from the nearly 8,000 works of art in the Brooks Collection.

Collection Highlights would not be possible without the generous support of the Arthur F. and Alice E. Adams Charitable Foundation. Sharing in the vision of the catalogue since its inception, the foundation's unparalleled investment made this publication a reality, not just a dream. This project is just one of many important museum initiatives that the foundation has supported. We are honored to have Renée Guibao serve as a valued trustee on the museum's board. The personal involvement and commitment of the Adams Foundation board members in the museum will enable the Brooks to expand its contributions to the cultural life of the community for years to come.

I am grateful to members of the Brooks Museum staff who have written about the objects in our collection: Dr. Walter R. Brown, adjunct curator of decorative arts; Kathy Dumlao, assistant curator of education; Karleen Gardner, associate curator of education; Marilyn Masler, associate registrar; Marina Pacini, chief curator; Ana Vejzovic, former assistant curator; and John Weeden, exhibitions manager. With perseverance and good humor, these authors have greatly expanded our understanding of the permanent collection. I am especially appreciative of the work of Marina Pacini, who diligently helped with the editing of all of the entries and the general coordination of the project. Claudia Towell, director of marketing, and Heather Klein, graphic designer, deserve immense appreciation for the design of this beautiful publication. I am grateful to Kip Peterson, collections manager, for coordinating the photography of all of the objects and facilitating access to the collection. Aiding in the photography of the works were Bert Sharpe, chief preparator, and Paul Tracy, associate preparator.

On behalf of all of the authors, I would like to thank the following individuals for their help with the *Collection Highlights*: Louisa Bann, Samantha Baskind, Ryan Byrne, Dee Garceau-Hagen, Douglas Halijan, Wil Hergenrader, Melanie Herzog, Earnestine Jenkins, Heidi King, Jim Lutz, Robert Mann, David McCarthy, Steven McKenzie, Jeff Nesin, David Nester, Michael Quick, Jim Ramsey, Murray Riss, Randy Roberts, David Robinson, Ted Rust, and Sylvia Yount. Finally, Carlisle Hacker deserves immense credit for her work as editor for the book.

Kaywin Feldman

Figure 1

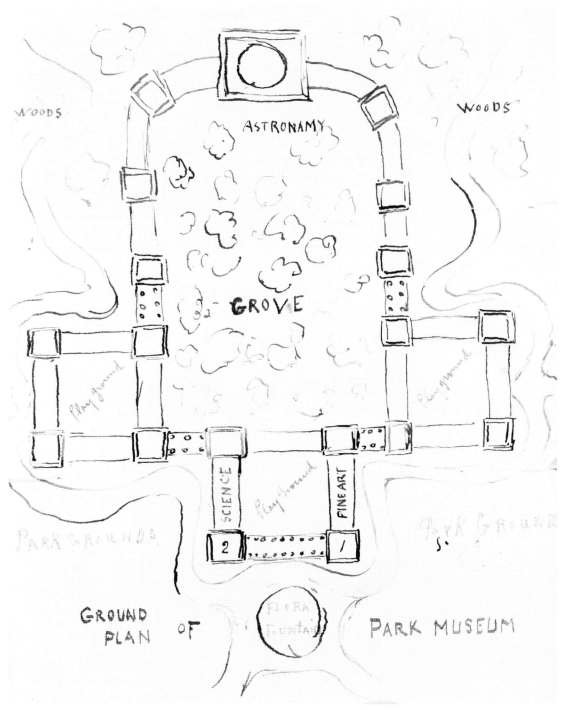

WOODS

WOODS

ASTRONAMY

GROVE

Playground

Playground

SCIENCE

Playground

FINE ART

2

1

PARK GROUNDS

PARK GROUNDS

FLORA Fountain

GROUND PLAN OF PARK MUSEUM

Figure 2

Ever Heedful of the Future:
A History of the Memphis Brooks Museum of Art

By 1900 Memphis had recovered from a devastating yellow fever epidemic and reestablished itself as a thriving commercial center. The town's burgeoning affluence fostered the establishment of civic institutions such as the Cossitt Library (1893) and the Overton Park Zoo (1906). Spearheaded by Mrs. E.A. Neely, a campaign was begun to found an art museum in Overton Park. Neely challenged the artist Carl Gutherz (1844-1907) to give form to her idea of an art museum in 1906. Gutherz's preliminary sketches detail a series of small pavilions dedicated to the arts, sciences, and humanities, connected by pergolas that enclosed playgrounds and gardens (see figure 2). He also drew a beautiful example of what one of the pavilions might look like (see figure 3). The resemblance of this small building to a mausoleum is not accidental, as Gutherz proposed that all of the pavilion buildings be constructed as memorials to deceased patrons. Both drawings were dashed off on the back of sheets of stationery.

In a letter to Neely of November 21, 1906, Gutherz expressed his desire to locate the museum where it would be most easily accessible and allow ample space for future growth.[1] He thought the architecture should be in perfect accord with the landscape and preservation of artwork should be the structure's primary goal. In his letter, Gutherz wrote "that Memphis is sadly in need of the refining influence of the esthetic is beyond dispute, and that the lack of it must be a canker in every true and intellectual citizen's heart: in fact, we cannot take our place among the intellectual cities of this or any other country without this consideration. Memphis has long outgrown its town swaddling clothes and donned its city affectation."

Under the auspices of the Park Museum Association, whose logo included images of children flanking a drawing of a squirrel holding a nut and the phrase "ever heedful of the future," Neely set out to raise broad support for an art museum. Her original plan involved raising money by the collection of discarded wastepaper by schoolchildren. The program evolved to engage first-grade children in the gathering of wastepaper on Mondays; second-grade children searched for linen and cotton rags on Tuesdays; and on Wednesdays third-grade students collected waste rubber (garden hoses, galoshes, pencil erasers, and buggy tires).

The Park Museum project languished until 1913 when Bessie Vance Brooks donated $100,000 to the City of Memphis to build a museum in honor of her late husband, Samuel Hamilton Brooks, who died in 1912. Originally from Ohio, Brooks moved to Memphis in 1858 and joined Brooks and McCall, his brother's wholesale grocery business. After fighting in the Confederate army for four years he formed Brooks-Neely wholesale

Figure 3

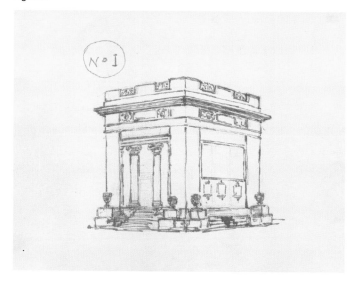

grocers, which prospered until the firm dissolved partnership in 1897 and Brooks retired. Bessie Vance, a member of a prominent Memphis family, became Brooks' second wife when they married in 1902. An artist, Vance traveled to Paris and studied under her lifelong friend Kate Carl, and was painted by Carl around 1890 (see figure 4).

Inspired by the plans laid by Neely, the wife of her husband's business partner, and Carl Gutherz, Mrs. Brooks hired the New York architect James Gamble Rogers to design a museum in 1913. Together they selected a grassy knoll in the southwest corner of Overton Park for the building. No stranger to Memphis, Rogers had recently completed the large Shelby County Courthouse (1905-1909) to great acclaim. Constructed of white Georgian marble, and designed in the Beaux Arts style, the museum building features a Serliana, a large central arched opening that is taller than the two flanking flat-topped openings. The Serliana is surrounded on either side by delicate bas-relief panels depicting personifications of painting and sculpture. Carved into a wooden panel over the door, a sign reads, "Put thou thy faith in the Lord and be [sic] doing good." Taking a large part of its inspiration from the Morgan Library in New York City, which was designed by the firm of McKim, Mead, and White, the museum soon became widely known as "the jewel box in the park."

Constructed at a cost of $115,000, the Brooks Memorial Art Gallery (Brooks) opened to the public on May 26, 1916 (see figure 5). At the dedication, Mrs. Brooks' speech was read by the Episcopal Bishop Thomas F. Gailor: "I hereby give and donate this building to the public use as a repository, conservatory, and museum of art—to be kept and maintained forever, under the care and regulation of the Park Commission and other authorities of the City of Memphis . . . for the free use and service of students of art and for the enjoyment, inspiration, and instruction of our people."

The museum opened without a collection, staff, or exhibition schedule. The Memphis Art Association, founded in 1914 by members of the Nineteenth Century Club, adopted the Brooks.[2] Florence McIntyre, an artist who studied under William Merritt Chase (see page 172) and was the Art Association's corresponding secretary, became the museum's first director. The inaugural exhibition secured by McIntyre and the Memphis Art Association opened on July 10, 1916, and included work by Frederick J. Waugh, Childe Hassam, Kate Carl, and Ben Foster.

Portraits by Cecilia Beaux of Samuel Hamilton Brooks and Bessie Vance Brooks were the first works of art to enter the permanent collection (see figures 6 and 7) in 1916. Beaux, a successful Philadelphia artist who studied at the Pennsylvania Academy of the Fine Arts, was commissioned by Mrs. Brooks in 1911 to paint her husband at Green Alley, the artist's summer home in Gloucester, Massachusetts. The companion portrait of Mrs. Brooks was also painted by Beaux in 1911. Until Mrs. Brooks' death in 1943, all acquisitions were approved by a small acquisitions committee that consisted of established artists. The first committee included Chase, Beaux, and Carl. Proposed acquisitions were sent to New York for the convenience of the committee.

Figure 4

The job of the acquisitions committee was not terribly onerous at this time since the collection grew initially at a slow rate—by 1941 the collection contained only twenty-one works. One of the museum's earliest acquisitions was Chase's *Self Portrait*, a gift of the Art Association in 1922 (see page 172). This painting was included in the 1917 Chase *Memorial Exhibition of Paintings*, which was on view at the Metropolitan Museum before it was sent to the Brooks.

In 1928 Samuel H. Kress made his first donation to the museum, a tondo depicting the Madonna and Child with Saint John, attributed at the time to Raffaelino de Garbo and currently considered to be the work of a Lorenzo di Credi follower. The gift was made in recognition of the opening of the first Kress store in Memphis in 1896. In December 1932, in the middle of the Great Depression, Kress loaned the Brooks fifty-three of the paintings in his collection for an exhibition that was so successful it drew 2,000 visitors on opening day. In 1933 Edward A. Bell's *Lady in Gray*, painted in 1889 (see page 154), entered the collection, a gift made by Bell at the urging of artist Irvin R. Wiles, a member of the museum's acquisitions committee and a friend of Chase's.

A variety of women's civic clubs and arts organizations supported the museum in its early years with their time and talent by hosting fund-raising events, lectures, concerts, children's programs, and meetings. These organizations included the Memphis Art League, the Memphis Garden Club, the Alpha Book Club, the Memphis Palette and Brush Club, and the American Association of University Women. The Brooks Memorial League was founded in 1934 with the purpose of "stimulating and promoting the interests and the work of the Brooks Memorial Art Gallery, with special attention focused on activities for children." Initially, membership was open to just twenty-five active members, but this number expanded to one hundred in 1955 and is unlimited today. From the beginning, the league strove to make art and art classes accessible to children of all ages through a variety of programs. An early project included the Motor Corps—women drivers who brought groups of children from schools to the museum. Known today as the Brooks Museum League, these dedicated women

Figure 6   Figure 7

continue to promote art education by hosting the annual *Mid-South Scholastic Art Awards* to honor exemplary art made by students in grades seven through twelve.

An integral part of other museum projects, the league established the docent program in 1965 and initiated and staffed the museum's first gift shop. With a long history of supporting acquisitions on behalf of the museum, in 1938 the league purchased a diorama of Donatello's studio made by Lorado Taft, and later added similar dioramas of Michelangelo's and Praxiteles' studios. Other acquisitions made possible by the league include Leon Koury's *The Compress Worker* (see page 202), John Rogers' *Coming to the Parson* (see page 142), and the *Torso of Pan* (see page 28).

In 1936 an art reference library opened that helped to further the museum's educational mission. The State Art Project of the Works Progress Administration gave the Brooks 12,000 reproductions of famous works of art that could be used by students and art teachers who had no other means of seeing these works.

The early exhibition schedule focused primarily on the work of American artists such as Robert Henri (see page 168), Childe Hassam (see page 150), Arthur B. Davies, John Sloan, and Rockwell Kent (all of whom are represented in the Brooks Collection). Most of the exhibitions hosted during this early period in the museum's history were organized by the American Federation of Arts (AFA). Anna Hyatt Huntington loaned the museum sixty-nine of her sculptures for an exhibition seen only in New Orleans and Memphis in 1937 (see figure 8). As a result of the exhibition, for which Huntington assumed all costs, she donated the sculpture *Greyhounds Playing* (see page 186) to the museum in 1938.

Between 1933 and 1957 a major annual exhibition was held in conjunction with Memphis Cotton Carnival. Memphis businessman and arts philanthropist I.L. "Ike" Myers, chair of the Cotton Carnival's Fine Arts Committee at the time, was instrumental in bringing major exhibitions to Memphis. He organized an exhibition of thirteen paintings by English painters and twenty-four paintings and forty etchings by American artists in 1938. One year later, the Cotton Carnival exhibition included paintings by Mexican artists, as well as European old masters, which drew a record 10,000 people in six days. Upon his death in 1960, Myers bequeathed the museum his collection, including Rembrandt etchings, Honoré Daumier lithographs, and paintings. (see figure 9)

In 1942 the City of Memphis purchased thirty-eight paintings and objets d'art for $30,000 from Warner S. McCall in St. Louis. Several collection highlights emerged from this purchase, including portraits by Sofonisba Anguissola (see page 64), Sir Anthony van Dyck (see page 72), and Sir Henry Raeburn (see page 102). Significant American paintings were also added, such as Winslow Homer's *Reading by the Brook* (see page 146) and *In the Campagna* by George W. Inness. At the time of this purchase, however, the press maligned Mayor Walter Chandler and Park Commission Chairman John B. Vesey for spending public money unwisely. So fervent was the civic debate about the purchase that a story ran in the March 6, 1944, issue of *Time* magazine declaring that "the City of Memphis has been stung." In an article in the April 21, 1944, *Memphis Press-Scimitar*, Helen Warden quoted "connoisseurs" as saying that the McCall Collection was "the most notorious lot of second-hand art ever unloaded on a museum."

The collection of works on paper was firmly established by Dr. Louis Levy, a notable physician who presented the Brooks with 1,010 prints in 1947. Levy began building his collection in the 1930s and 1940s when he subscribed to the Associated American Artists (AAA) mail subscription for prints. The bulk of his collection consisted of lithographs by AAA artists, such as Thomas Hart Benton, Grant Wood, and John Steuart Curry. His gift also included prints by European artists such as Lucas van Leyden, Rembrandt van Rijn, Adriaen van Ostade, and Honoré Daumier. In the years

Figure 8

Figure 9

since Levy's gift, the print collection has grown to more than 4,000 works, especially through the gifts of the Armand Hammer Foundation, Myers, Milton M. Adams, AutoZone Inc., and the Madonna Circle. An extensive collection of artists' books was given in 1990 by local collectors Isabel Ehrlich and Charles F. Goodman.

In 1952 the Samuel H. Kress Foundation announced that it would give Memphis a collection of European masterpieces as part of its national initiative to donate more than 700 old master paintings and sculptures to regional American art museums. To receive this significant gift, the foundation stipulated that the Brooks Memorial Art Gallery had to expand in order to accommodate the collection. The new 15,000-square-foot addition, designed by Memphis architect Everett Woods and constructed at the cost of $250,000, opened to the public in 1955 (see figure 10). This utilitarian single-story building clad in rough-cut stone included a basement and nine exhibition galleries, all of which were air-conditioned. The expansion also gave the Brooks a kitchen, offices, a lounge, and an auditorium.

The opening exhibition in the new building included thirty-one paintings from the 16th to the 20th centuries belonging to Memphis philanthropists Lillian and Morrie Moss. Over the next thirty years, the Mosses frequently loaned part of their collection for temporary exhibitions, such as the 1965 *Selected Paintings from the Mr. and Mrs. Morrie A. Moss Collection: A Loan Exhibition*, which displayed thirty-eight paintings from the 17th to the 19th centuries. Starting in 1954, they also made frequent donations of art, including outstanding Dutch, Flemish, and British paintings, silver, sculpture, and decorative arts. Highlights from the Moss collection include William-Adolphe Bouguereau's *Au Pied de la Falaise* (see page 114), Richard Wilson's *Tivoli: Temple of the Sibyl and the Campagna* (see page 94), John Hoppner's *A Country Girl*, George Romney's *Portrait of Lady Wright* (see page 100), and Jan van Goyen's *River Scene* (see page 76). A close associate of Armand Hammer's, Morrie Moss was also instrumental in the exhibition of eighty-two paintings from Hammer's collection in 1967, which attracted more than 50,000 visitors. The Mosses' impact on the collection's growth continues today due to the Moss acquisition endowment fund established in 1984.

Mildred Hudson, Nancy Glazer, Adele Lemm, Marjorie Liebman, and Dorothy Sturm—a visionary group of women committed to the appreciation and promotion of contemporary art—formed Art Today in 1953. An influential support group of the museum, Art Today sponsored contemporary art lectures and organized contemporary exhibitions such as the 1953 *Betty Parsons Group*, which included artwork by Theodore Stamos, Ad Reinhardt, Richard Pousette-Dart, Marjorie Liebman (whose work is represented in the Brooks Collection), and Alfonso Ossorio. In 1957 Art Today made its first gifts to the collection: six silk screens by Jackson Pollock (see page 212), Theodore Stamos' *Oriental Beggar*, and *Moon Steps* by Kenzo Okado. Art Today began taking "off the wall" trips to New York City in 1983 to purchase works for the collection. In its fifty-year history, Art Today has added many modern works to the permanent collection, such as Georgia O'Keeffe's *Waterfall—No.1—Iao Valley—Maui* (see page 190), Josef Albers' *Study for Homage to the Square: Young Voice* (see page 218), Elizabeth Murray's *The Tempest* (see page 250), Ansel Adams' *Moonrise, Hernandez, New Mexico* (see page 200), and Alan Shields' *Cat Nip Tabs*.

Under the leadership of Louise Bennett Clark, the Brooks maintained a close and beneficial relationship with the Samuel H. Kress Foundation. Clark assumed the director's position from Valerie Farrington in 1933 and held this position until she retired in 1961. She remains the Brooks' longest-serving director. During her tenure, Clark oversaw the acquisition of the McCall, Levy, and Kress collections, as well as the erection of the new building. Although the possibility of the Kress gift was announced in 1952, it was not until 1961 that all of the thirty-two works given by the foundation were received. Ranging in date from Rinaldo da Siena's *Madonna and Child with Four Saints* in 1265 (see page 44) to Canaletto's *The Grand Canal from Campo di San Vio* in 1785 (see page 90), the Kress Collection offers an excellent survey of artwork from the Sienese, Florentine, and Venetian schools. In the years that have passed since its initial gift, the foundation has generously supported conservation, research, and publications on this significant part of the Brooks Collection.

Like much of Memphis, Overton Park, and all of the institutions located inside of it, was a segregated institution. African Americans were permitted to enter the park only on Thursdays. At ten o'clock in the morning on Tuesday, March 22, 1960, four African American men and three African American women, all students at LeMoyne-Owen College, entered the Brooks Memorial Art Gallery to view the *Mid-South Art Exhibit*. Another six African American students remained outside the building. All of the students were arrested and charged by the city with disorderly conduct and loitering. The seven students who entered the building were also charged by the state with threatened breach of the peace. On December 2, 1960, it was announced by the Park Commission that the Brooks Memorial Art Gallery was desegregated.

In 1950 the city approved the appointment by the Park Commission of nine prominent businessmen as trustees to direct the museum's operations. The first female trustee was elected in 1969 to a fifteen-member board. Park Commission management was terminated in 1970 and replaced by the Arts and Sciences Commission, reporting to the mayor. Eventually, members of the board were appointed by the mayor and approved by the City Council to manage public funds and establish policy. In 1957 the private Fine Arts Foundation was formed to allow the museum to raise money for collections and programs through the subscription of memberships. Both boards were maintained separately until 1983.

Between 1952 and 1960 Hugo Dixon, a dedicated member of the museum's board who worked diligently with Clark to secure the Kress Foundation gift, gave the museum thirteen paintings from his extensive collection. Originally from Southport, England, Dixon and his wife, Margaret Oates Dixon, amassed a fine collection of British portraits and gave the museum Sir Joshua Reynolds' portrait *Mrs. Way* in 1954 and Sir Henry Raeburn's *Alexander Home* in 1962. The bulk of the Dixons' gift includes an impressive collection of French 19th-century paintings, including Camille Pissarro's *La Sente de Justice, Pontoise* (see page 112), Alfred Sisley's *Le Pont d'Argenteuil* (see page 110), Pierre-Auguste Renoir's *L'Ingenue*, and Édouard Vuillard's *Vue en Suisse* (see page 116). Other collection highlights given by the Dixons include Vanvitelli's *View of the Piazza del Popolo* (see page 82) and Luca Giordano's *The Slaying of the Medusa* (see page 80). After Hugo Dixon's death in 1974 the Dixon Gallery and Gardens opened in the Dixons' stately former home and grounds.

In 1959 the Memphis Academy of Arts, known since 1985 as the Memphis College of Art, moved to its dramatic new building, designed by Roy Harrover of Mann and Harrover. Adjacent to the Brooks in Overton Park, the physical proximity of the buildings further cemented the institutions' close relationship. The long history of collaboration began with the same sponsoring organization, the Memphis Art Association, and the same founding director, Florence McIntyre. In 1936 most of the students and faculty deserted the James Lee Memorial Academy of Arts and McIntyre's rigid devotion to the academic tradition and founded the new Memphis Academy of Arts. The museum and art

Figure 11

Figure 12

college have collaborated throughout their histories, jointly bringing artists such as Max Beckmann, Will Barnet, Tony Smith, and, more recently, Willie Cole to jury exhibitions, teach classes, and give public lectures. The Brooks Collection includes many works by Memphis College of Art professors, such as Burton Callicott (see page 188), Veda Reed, Henry Easterwood, Edwin C. Rust, Dolph Smith, Edward Faiers, and Dorothy Sturm.

The Little Garden Club was one of the Brooks Memorial Art Gallery's devoted support groups that worked hard to improve the surrounding landscape. The club developed the intimate Holly Court garden, located on the north side of the 1916 building and maintained today by the Brooks League. In 1962 the club presented the museum with sculptures by Wheeler Williams of three of the seasons: *Spring, Summer, and Fall.* Carved of Carrara marble and standing more than six feet tall, they were originally placed in niches designed for them along the south side of the 1955 building. They were moved to their current location on the south side of the 1916 building in 1998 (see figure 11). Along with *Winter*, these three sculptures were first made in fired porcelain as *The Four Seasons of Life* or *The Life of the Iris* and awarded a gold medal at the Paris *Exposition Internationale des Arts et Techniques dans la vie Moderne* in 1937. Although there was not enough space outside the building for *Winter*, in 1962 the artist donated the smaller-scale bronze model that was created in 1934. The Little Garden Club funded the addition of a set of marble stairs, designed by Everett Woods, leading up the hillside to the 1916 building entrance in 1968.

Carl Gutherz (see figure 12), who helped conceive the museum's original plans, continued to exert a strong influence on the Brooks. Although born in Switzerland, Gutherz spent his childhood and early adult years in Memphis. He subsequently went back to Europe, where he studied at the École des Beaux-Arts in Paris and traveled to Munich and Rome. He returned to the States from his second trip to Paris in 1896, when he was commissioned to paint the murals for the reading room of the Library of Congress. In two gifts made between 1968 and 1986, the artist's son, Marshall Goodheart, donated 155 paintings and 573 drawings by his father to the Brooks. The Gutherz Collection includes work from nearly every phase of the artist's career. The collection also contains Gutherz's letters, two handwritten journals, photographs, medals, and notes made about his works. The paintings include portraits of sitters like Susan B. Anthony and Gutherz's daughter, Godfriede; French and American landscapes; history paintings like *Bering Sea Arbitration*; and elaborate allegories such as *Light of the Incarnation* (see page 152).

When photographer and concert pianist Eugenia Buxton Whitnel died in 1971, she left the Brooks $250,000, the largest bequest received to that date. Jack Whitlock, who became director in 1972, used the funds to acquire significant works of art by 20th-century American artists such as Walt Kuhn (see page 208), Reginald Marsh (see page 194), Arthur Dove (see page 182), Arthur B. Davies, Jacques Lipchitz (see page 210), Thomas Hart Benton (see page 180), George Ault, and Ben Shahn (see page 222). During his tenure, Whitlock secured the Brooks' first accreditation from the American Association of Museums and completed the new addition to the museum that had been started by his predecessor, Robert McKnight.

Figure 13

The new building, which opened in 1973, was designed by the Memphis architectural firm Walk Jones + Francis Mah, Inc. and constructed for $850,000 (see figures 13 and 14). A Modernist building with Brutalist elements, such as the use of raw concrete and exposed structure, the building echoes Louis Kahn's use of concrete in his museums at Yale University in New Haven, Connecticut, and the Kimbell Art Museum in Fort Worth, Texas. Also incorporating notions of universal space as espoused by Ludwig Mies van der Rohe, the building originally called for the display of paintings on cable-hung cubes and planes. While innovative at the time, the system proved impractical and the space was significantly modified in the 1990s.

In 1979, under the leadership of Jay Gates, the museum's support groups—the Brooks Art Gallery League, Art Today, and the Brooks Memorial Art Gallery Foundation—were reorganized and each was incorporated with its own board of directors. In 1980, a new support group, the Decorative Arts Trust (DAT), was formed. The museum's decorative arts collection, already strong with earlier gifts from the Memphis Glass Collectors Club and the Norcross collection of English Lustreware, has expanded greatly with the DAT's generosity. Additions to the collection secured with the assistance of the DAT are *The Mocking of Christ* stained glass (see page 54), the Spanish *Processional Cross* (see page 48), the Mallard *Chest of Drawers* (see page 132), the Tiffany & Co. *Pair of Ewers* (see page 156), and the Frank Lloyd Wright *Chair* (see page 162). The DAT also hosts seminars, lectures, and events to expand the appreciation and understanding of decorative arts in Memphis. The trust's promotion of the decorative arts has inspired collectors to make donations to the collection, such as the twenty-nine pieces of Fitzhugh-pattern Chinese export porcelain donated by Nathan Dermon in 1998 and Dr. William Huckaba's 1999 bequest of a fine 18th-century English walnut longcase clock made by John Wait.

The decorative arts collection increased after receipt of the Isenberg bequest in 1987. Julie Isenberg, a graduate of Smith College who was committed to civil rights and social justice, was also keenly interested in books, music, and art. Today part of the Brooks Collection, Childe Hassam's etching *Tree* was Isenberg's first purchase, acquired with money given to her by her parents as a wedding gift. Several important pieces of American furniture Isenberg acquired became part of her bequest to the Brooks, including a Queen Anne *High Chest of Drawers* (see page 126), the Goddard *Tallcase Clock* (see page128), and a New York Federal period dining table. She also donated drawings, prints, and paintings by Maurice de Vlaminck and Maurice Utrillo (see page 118).

The 1980s brought extensive administrative changes to the museum, a succession of directors, and a beautiful new building addition. In 1983 the museum changed its name to the Memphis Brooks Museum of Art, Inc., and in 1989 the Brooks separated from city government and became a fully private institution. The City of Memphis, however, continues to own the museum's building and the bulk of the collection acquired prior to 1989.

In 1986, following a yearlong master plan study, the firm of Skidmore, Owings, and Merrill (SOM) was selected to design the third major expansion of the institution (see figure 15). The project was led by architect Richard Keating of SOM's Houston office, in association with the local firm Askew, Nixon, Ferguson & Wolfe. The Postmodern-influenced design received a prestigious award from *Progressive Architecture* magazine. Taking the form and details of the original 1916 building as its point of departure, the expansion replaced the earlier 1955 addition and created a new entrance and public face for the museum. At a cost of $6.5 million, this new addition added important amenities: a new entry rotunda, restaurant, gift shop, and lecture theater, as well as desperately needed galleries and collection storage.

The new millennium was marked by the donation of 227 works of art from the corporate collection of AutoZone, Inc. in 2001. The collection, formed under the extraordinary vision of Memphis philanthropist and business leader J.R. "Pitt" Hyde III, includes paintings, photographs, prints, drawings, and sculpture, primarily by artists living and working in the South. The AutoZone Collection expanded the museum's already strong holdings of important photographers working in the South, such as William Eggleston (see page 238) and William Christenberry (see page 240), as well as adding sculpture by William Edmondson (see page 196) and prints by Elizabeth Catlett (see page 206).

In 1933 the Brooks Collection contained nineteen paintings by mostly American artists housed in a building of 8,200 square feet. Today, that collection has expanded to nearly 8,000 works of art, including painting, sculpture, works on paper, decorative arts, and video art from most major world cultures—housed in an 86,000-square-foot facility. Thanks to the generosity of countless donors and collectors, the collection and institution continue to grow, ever heedful of the future.

Kaywin Feldman

Figure 14

Figure 15

Endnotes

The sources used in this essay include scrapbooks from the museum's archives, notes from Brooks family members, board meeting minutes, and museum newsletters.

1. This letter is part of the Gutherz collection at the Brooks Museum.

2. Florence McIntyre, *Art and Life* (Memphis: Florence M. McIntyre, 1952), p. 9.

Figures

1. Unknown Photographer
   Schilling Gallery with niche surrounding *Portrait of Samuel Hamilton Brooks* by Cecilia Beaux, ca. 1920
   Memphis Brooks Museum of Art Photograph Archives

2. **Carl Gutherz**, American (b. Switzerland), 1844-1907
   Ground Plan, Park Museum Proposal, November 1906
   Ink on letterhead stationery
   Gift of Marshall and Elizabeth Goodheart 1986

3. **Carl Gutherz**, American (b. Switzerland), 1844-1907
   Detail of Pavilion, Park Museum Proposal, November 1906
   Ink on letterhead stationery
   Gift of Marshall and Elizabeth Goodheart 1986

4. Katherine "Kate" Augusta Carl, American, ca. 1850 -1938
    Portrait of Bessie Vance Brooks, ca. 1890
    Oil on canvas, 48 1/8" x 34" (122.2 cm x 86.5 cm)
    Gift of Mrs. Samuel Hamilton Brooks 16.4

5. Unknown Photographer
    1916 building from the southeast corner, ca. 1960
    Memphis Brooks Museum of Art Photograph Archives

6. Cecilia Beaux, American, 1855-1942
    Portrait of Mr. Samuel Hamilton Brooks, 1911
    Oil on canvas, 39" x 29 1/8" (99 cm x 73.7 cm)
    Gift of Mrs. Samuel Hamilton Brooks 16.2

7. Cecilia Beaux, American, 1855-1942
    Portrait of Mrs. Samuel Hamilton Brooks, 1911
    Oil on canvas, 47 3/4" x 35" (121.2 cm x 88.9 cm)
    Gift of Mrs. Samuel Hamilton Brooks 16.1

8. Unknown Photographer
    1916 building foyer with Anna Hyatt Huntington's *Greyhounds Playing,* ca. 1940
    Memphis Brooks Museum of Art Photograph Archives

9. Sir Jacob Epstein, British (b. United States), 1880-1959
    Head of Isaac L. Myers, ca. 1948
    Bronze, 13" x 6 3/4" x 8 1/4" (33 cm x 17 cm x 21 cm)
    Gift of the Artist 50.11

10. Unknown Photographer
    The 1955 building from the northeast corner, ca. 1955
    Memphis Brooks Museum of Art Photograph Archives

11. Wheeler Williams, American, 1897-1972
    Spring, Summer, and Fall, 1961
    Carrara marble, 81" x 28" x 16" (205.7 cm x 53.3 cm x 40.6 cm) each
    Gift of the Little Garden Club 62.14.112.
    Photograph: David Nester Studio

12. Charles Alfred Zimmerman, American (b. Austria), 1844-1909
    Portrait of Carl Gutherz, ca. 1884
    Silver gelatin print, 5 9/16" x 3 7/8" (14.1 cm x 9.8 cm)
    Gift of Marshall and Elizabeth Goodheart 86.22.581

13. Unknown Photographer
    The 1973 building from the northeast corner, ca. 1973
    Memphis Brooks Museum of Art Photograph Archives

14. Unknown Photographer
    The 1973 building's interior, ca. 1973
    Memphis Brooks Museum of Art Photograph Archives

15. Jeffrey Jacobs/Sims Studios
    Twilight exterior view of the Memphis Brooks Museum of Art
    Copyright 1990 Jeffrey Jacobs/Sims Studios

The Patera Painter
South Italian (Apulia)
Red-Figure Volute-Krater, ca. 340-320 B.C.E.
Painted terra-cotta
23" x 13 1/2" x 11 1/8" (58.4 cm x 34.3 cm x 28.3 cm)
Gift of the Director's Council 94.2

The Patera Painter's workshop was probably located in the Apulian city of Canosa. His name is derived from the frequency with which he depicted a long-handled *patera*—a wide, shallow vessel used for pouring libations over a grave—within the scenes on his vases. Appropriately, a majority of the surviving vessels attributed to the Patera Painter illustrate funerary scenes, set either in a *naiskos*, a shrine-like structure erected for the deceased, or at a grave stela (tomb marker). Apulian vases are divided into two distinct categories, the Plain style and the Ornate style, identified by the manner in which they are decorated. As seen here, the Ornate style is defined by funerary and mythological scenes rendered on large vases such as kraters and amphorae. Such scenes typically include numerous figures in complex compositions, embellished with elaborate pattern work and floral decoration, and enlivened by a substantial amount of added color, primarily white, yellow, and red.

The obverse of this Ornate-style volute-krater, a vessel used for mixing wine with water, portrays a young woman seated on a stool inside a *naiskos*. Holding a large box called a *cista* in her left hand and a mirror in her right, the figure is illustrated in added white to delineate that she is the sculptural representation of the deceased. Two female figures flank the *naiskos* and bring offerings to the dead, such as a *phiale* (plate), mirrors, and grapes. On the neck of the vessel, intricately spiraling tendrils frame a profile female head emerging from the blossom of a large bell-shaped flower, all applied in added color. Carved in relief, the volutes on the handles of the obverse are ornamented with female heads with curly yellow hair, and on the reverse, female heads with curly black hair. The principal scene on the reverse depicts a grave stela approached on either side by a woman bearing offerings. Funerary scenes such as these were often commissioned on large Ornate-style vessels that were frequently left as monuments in a wealthy family's chamber tomb.

KHD

China
Western Han Dynasty (206 B.C.E.-C.E. 25)
Horse and Rider, 1st century
Polychrome earthenware
14 7/8" x 13 1/8" x 4 3/4" (37.8 cm x 33.3 cm x 12.1 cm)
Gift of the Director's Council; funds provided by the Lula Coffey Bequest 2000.4

One of ancient China's most prosperous periods was the Han dynasty. During this time literature and the arts flourished. Confucianism was reestablished as the official ideology and these renewed beliefs encouraged the use of small models in burials, replacing the earlier practice of human and animal sacrifice. The Chinese tradition of elaborate entombment continued, and replicas of material possessions, animals, and people were placed in tombs to accompany and serve the deceased in the afterlife. Usually formed from clay or wood, these representative objects, called *ming ch'i*, often depicted servants, musicians, farmworkers, jugglers, elaborate houses, watchtowers, watchdogs, barns, granaries, pigpens, fowl, and horses.

Tian ma, or celestial horses, came to symbolize prestige, power, and wealth during the Han dynasty. Described as superlative in every way, this new breed of horse was brought from Fergana (a present-day province of Russian Turkestan) to China by Han emperor Wu Di (141- 87 B.C.E.) to enable his armies to fight invading equestrian soldiers. Horse and equestrian sculptures became essential elements in the furnishing of important tombs. Modeled in clay, this horse with a neatly hogged mane, a docked tail, and erect ears is typically Ferganan in style—fat, strong, and powerfully built with slender limbs. Ready for battle, the rider sits erect in the saddle, wearing a headdress, a short padded robe, and, on his back, a small quiver, in which arrows might have been placed originally. His garments are elaborately painted in cinnabar, black, and white. The black body of the horse is contrasted with the bright green, vermilion, blue, and white of the saddle blanket and trappings. At one time miniature reins made of rope, cloth, or metal were probably looped through the holes in the horse's mouth and the rider's hands. This polychrome equestrian figure signifies the Han dynasty fascination with horses, as well as the importance these animals served in the military and the afterlife.

KVG

Greco-Roman
Torso of Pan, 1st century B.C.E. - C.E. 2nd century
Marble
18 1/2" x 15" x 8" (47 cm x 38.1 cm x 20.3 cm)
Gift of the Brooks League 89.42

In 211 B.C.E., the Roman General Marcellus, conqueror of the exceptionally wealthy Greek city of Syracuse, returned to Rome not only with the usual spoils of war, but also with the finest examples of art. Following Marcellus' introduction of Greek art, the Romans enthusiastically began collecting it, and if a particular Greek original was unobtainable, a copy was commissioned. Most Greek sculpture was originally cast in bronze, but when several copies were requested, Roman artists often employed marble, a less expensive material. After the copies were carved, the original bronze sculptures were often melted down and the metal used for military purposes. The *Torso of Pan* dates to the Greco-Roman period (30 B.C.E.-C.E. 312), suggesting it is likely a Roman copy of a Greek original.

Pan was the mischievous god of the forest and meadows, worshipped in ancient times by shepherds who wanted their flocks to flourish. He had the legs, horns, and tail of a goat; the body of a man; and a long shaggy beard. Scholars identify the subject of this piece as the Greek god Pan, primarily from the small tail located at the base of the spine. Additional evidence comes from the resemblance to two complete sculptures—located in the Museo Archeologico Nazionale in Naples and the Museo Nazionale in Rome—of Pan teaching a young student to play the pipes. It is likely that the Brooks sculpture would also have been part of a similar sculptural group; however, its original composition is unknown.

The torso is captured in a twisting motion with a forward bend at the waist. Pan's left shoulder extends upward while his right dips down, counterbalanced by the opposite movement of his hips. The result is a series of small creases of skin on the lower left side of the sculpture and a broad sweep of musculature on the right. From behind, the curve of the body appears more pronounced in the arc of the spine and the frontward roll of the shoulders. The exquisite torso exemplifies the Greek admiration of the human form. The exaggeration of movement, sweeping lines, and strong contrast of light and shadow are all characteristics of Hellenistic art (323-30 B.C.E.), which was especially prized and frequently copied by the Romans.

KHD

Pre-Columbian
Remojadas (Veracruz, Mexico)
Standing Female Figure, ca. 500-900
Painted terra-cotta
22 3/8" x 21" x 5" (56.8 cm x 53.3 cm x 12.7 cm)
Gift of the Director's Council 95.1.2

The pre-Columbian culture referred to as Remojadas developed along the central-southern coast of the Gulf of Mexico, beginning ca. 150. The name Remojadas references the specific site in an area just west of the modern city of Veracruz, where a wide range of ceramic figures has been found. The Remojadas style is an eclectic one, perhaps because the ancient site lay on a trade route between many other Mexican cultures, providing multiple artistic influences. The figures' heads were often made in molds and the bodies were hand-built, a technique introduced from Teotihuacán. The sculptures frequently function as whistles, with a hole in the foot or head, though no such evidence can be found on this example.

Closely resembling the Upper Remojadas style, which is characterized by animated figures dressed in elaborate appliqued costumes and headdresses, this standing female figure wears a tightly fitted two-piece garment and a splendid chin-strap headdress. Standing with her arms outstretched in a supplicating gesture, she confronts the viewer with her wide eyes and fixed gaze. Her oversized head is covered in a light ocher slip of clay that contrasts with the rougher, porous clay of the rest of her form. Painted in black asphalt, her mouth is slightly open. Now empty, her ear spools may have once been ornamented with an inlay of a precious material that has since been lost, and her wrists are adorned with simple bands. Her plain garment is decorated with bows on the bodice and at the waist of her skirt. Braided ribbons and loops at her hips add further ornamentation to the skirt. While the specific purpose of this sculpture is unknown, she may represent a deity, a priestess, a performer, or perhaps a victim of sacrifice.

KHD

China
Tang Dynasty (618-907)
Head of a Guardian (Lokapala)
Sandstone
10 1/8" x 7 5/8" x 7 3/4" (25.7 cm x 19.4 cm x 19.7 cm)
Memphis Brooks Museum of Art Purchase; funds provided
by Lula Coffey Bequest 2000.5

The Tang dynasty, regarded as one of China's most glorious eras, is referred to as the Golden Age. Patronage of the Tang emperors and the general wealth of the period encouraged the development of the visual arts and poetry. Although Taoism was the official religion of the imperial house, Buddhism, which came to China with missionaries from India and central Asia on the Silk Road, was also practiced. Buddhist art flourished and cult images of *Lokapala*, or heavenly kings, gradually took hold in the sixth century and came to prominence in the Tang dynasty.

The iconography of the guardian king standing upon demons or animals was regarded as so potent a symbol of protection against evil that it was readily adopted by the Chinese. Many of these figures were made of clay and others, like this one, were carved in stone and placed in pairs at the entrance of tombs. Sculpted in fine-grained reddish brown sandstone, this head of a *Lokapala* was originally part of a complete figure, dressed in armor, in a defiant pose. Because of their Buddhist origin and the Chinese belief that Western features were more frightening, the sculptors gave many of these guardians foreign characteristics. With a bold, fearsome expression, the head has bulging eyes fixed in a steady gaze under arched eyebrows, a large aquiline nose, and a mouth with tightly closed, well-formed lips that are flanked by deep ridges curving down to a broad chin. He wears a helmet carved to represent modeled leather with a tuft of fur on top and rounded scroll motifs on the front; the lower edge is folded back to form a double layer ending in a thick roll at ear level. With his defiant appearance, the *Lokapala* symbolizes the unchallenged spiritual majesty of a heavenly king who served to protect the tomb against evil forces and grave robbers.

KVG

Colima, Mexico
Dog Effigy Vessel, 250 B.C.E-C.E. 400
Polished terra-cotta
9 1/4" x 16" x 7 1/2" (23.5 cm x 48.6 cm x 19.1 cm)
Gift of Dr. Rushton E. Patterson Jr. 96.6.1

Dog Effigy Vessel was found at an ancient burial site in the Colima region on the Pacific coast of western Mexico. Although lacking the spectacular pyramids of other pre-Columbian Mexican societies, until about 600 the peoples of Colima built elaborate underground tombs where the dead would be surrounded by objects used in life such as axes, jewelry, cutting blades, and a variety of ceramic goods. This vessel represents a hairless dog, indigenous to meso-America and cultivated in western Mexico, known as a *xoloitzcuintli* (as later named by the Aztecs). They were bred for companionship, protection, and food, which this ceramic dog would also symbolize for the deceased in the afterlife. An ancient breed, *xoloitzcuintlis* were believed to have descended from survivors of a disastrous world flood in pre-Columbian Mexican mythology. Its story reflects the importance of dogs to humans throughout the ages. Known today as the Chihuahua, this animal has become a potent symbol of Mexican cultural identity.

The figure's short and plump physique is intentionally exaggerated to the point of distortion, a characteristic of Colima-area potters, who favored stylistic caricature over faithful naturalism. Hand modeled rather than carved, effigy pots of this sort were made of highly burnished red clay, which resulted in a bright polish that still shines after so many centuries. Its standing pose is that of the obedient pet awaiting its master's command. Ears held high and eyes wide open, it appears alert and poised for action.

AV & JW

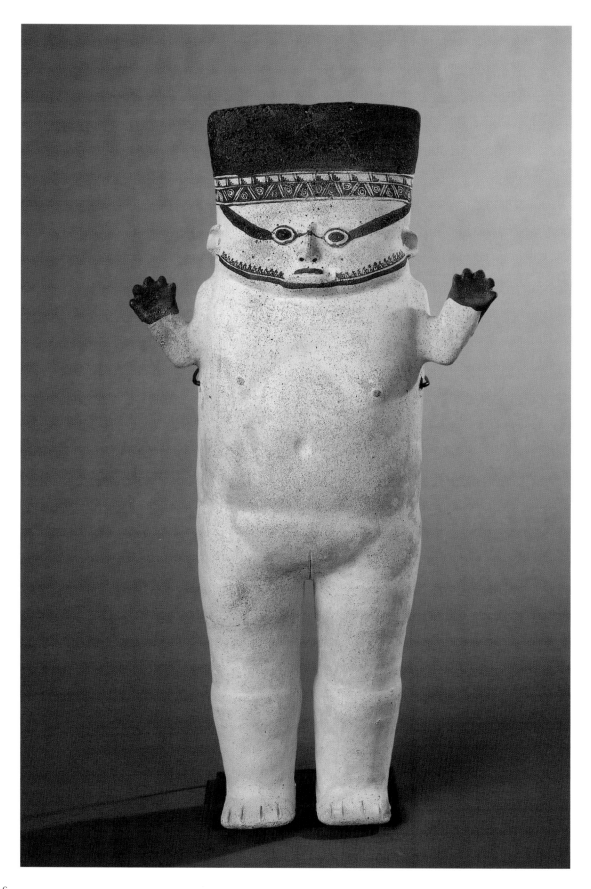

Chancay
Peru (Central Coast)
Standing Figure, ca. 1000-1400
Painted terra-cotta
25 1/4" x 13" x 6 3/4" (64.1 cm x 33 cm x 17.2 cm)
Gift of Dr. Rushton E. Patterson Jr. 95.3

Chancay was the most important city of the ancient Cuismancu Empire. A pre-Columbian people of the central coastal region of Peru, the Cuismancu were conquered by the Incas in the mid-1400s. Their use of standardized pottery molds made possible the production of vast quantities of ceramic objects. *Standing Figure* is a typical example of the *cuchimilco* form. Its raised arms with open, front-facing palms, signify the use of these figurines as devotional objects honoring Cuismancu gods in funerary rituals. Found exclusively at grave sites, these votive effigies are primarily female.

Her anatomy consists of the hand-drawn details of a navel, breasts, and a vagina, and simple marks in the clay to delineate the toes of each foot. Nostrils and ears are indicated with individual holes punctured into the clay. The heels have been intentionally extended to enable the object to stand upright in an earthen crypt. Decorative geometric patterns wrap around the headband of the squared, black headdress and beneath the chin line. Black pigment also accentuates the eyes, nose, and mouth in dramatic fashion. Paint dripping down the left arm and onto the left leg emphasizes the handmade quality of the object, its imperfection making evident the trace of the original creator centuries ago.

AV & JW

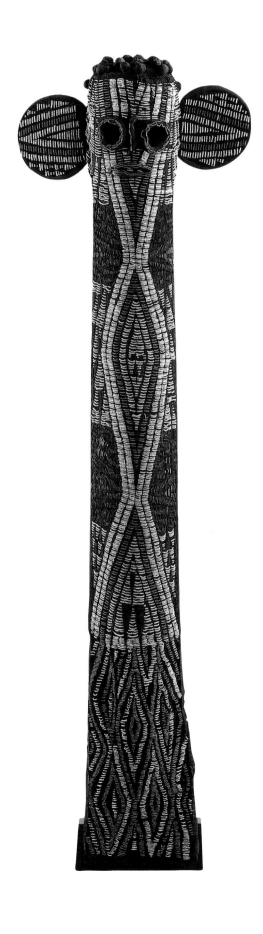

Bamileke
Africa, Cameroon
Elephant Society Mask, late 19th century
Raffia, beads, canvas
62 3/4" x 18 1/2" x 8 1/4" (159.4 cm x 47 cm x 21 cm)
Gift of the Director's Council 97.2.1

The Bamileke people live in a mountainous area of western Cameroon divided into several kingdoms, each ruled by a *fon*, or king. The elephant, esteemed for its power and bravery, is the revered symbol of chiefs and kings, and variously represents their authority, wealth, and military strength. Bamileke kings are thought to possess the supernatural power of transmutation by which they may take on the form of the elephant at will to perform legendary deeds. Just as an actual elephant can easily move a giant tree blocking its way, for example, so too is the king thought to be able to overcome great obstacles as the leader of his people. Members of the secret, all-male Elephant Mask Society, known as the Kuosi, wear extravagantly beaded masks when dancing during important ceremonies and the funerals of fellow society members. Historically, the ritual dance was also performed after victorious battles to display Bamileke power and intimidate defeated enemies.

The *Elephant Society Mask* is made of a strong, palm-derived fiber called raffia, and is festooned with white, maroon, and turquoise glass beads. This mask would have been worn as a part of a more elaborate costume while a drum and gong played and its wearer circled slowly on bare feet, letting the ears of the mask flap around him. Outfitted with a circular hat of bright red parrot feathers, robes of indigo and white *ndop* cloth trimmed with highly prized colobus monkey fur, beaded fly whisks, rattle anklets, and occasionally a leopard skin worn over the back, the dancer would have presented a spectacular and imposing sight to onlookers. The mask features a trunk; stiff, round ears characteristic of the African elephant; and a stylized human face covered in beads arrayed in geometric patterns that produce the effect of a whirling kaleidoscope of color as the dance progresses.[1] Knotted balls of dark canvas cloth on the top of the head represent human hair, accentuating a metaphorical association of the dancer's human-elephant hybrid persona while wearing the mask.

AV & JW

[1] Fred Johnson and Susan Rapchak, *African Art in the Ball State University Museum of Art: Materials for the Classroom* (Muncie, IN: Ball State University Museum of Art, 1998), p. 30.

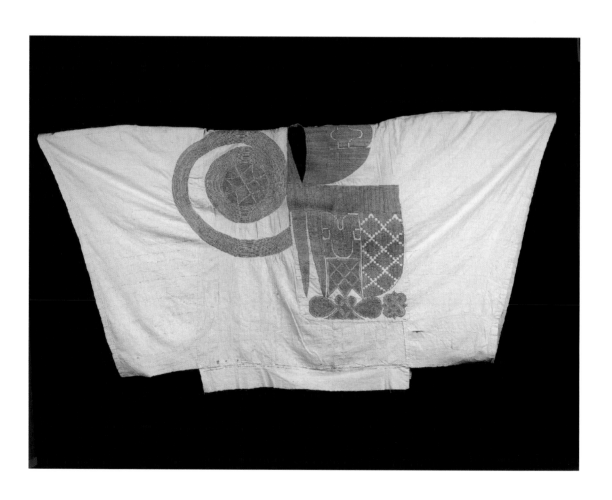

Hausa
Africa (Central Sudan and Nigeria)
Royal Robe with Two Knives Design and Insignias, late 19th to
early 20th century
Hand-spun cotton with wild silk embroidery
55"x 100" (139.7 cm x 256.5 cm)
Memphis Brooks Museum of Art Purchase 94.4

The Hausa, whose predominant religion is Islam, are an ethnic group living mainly in northern Nigeria and southern Niger. Their weavers are famous for embroidered robes that have the sides carefully gathered on the shoulders, and are worn over pantaloons. Called a *babba riga* or "great robe," this type of gown is worn by male leaders and dignitaries. Hausa dress, which has disseminated across west Africa, is worn by many people outside the Muslim sphere as a sign of status among men.

Male weavers make these robes on narrow-band treadle looms from cotton or silk strips, which are sewn together, folded, and then stitched along the sides. A *malan*, or learned man, then decorates the fabric by sewing geometric patterns, in the form of spirals and triangular motifs, which interlace on the front and back panels of the gown. The embroidered symbols function like an amulet, a protective object that is usually hidden and derives its power from the mystic knowledge concealed within it. The two knives motif, which represents protection, was probably borrowed from Islamic imagery, in which traditional designs are the "eight knives" and "two knives." The squares, typical Islamic symbols of the power of God and his creations, represent the four corners of the earth. The division of the square and its placement within the circle refers to the "magic square," a sacred numerological system that has been practiced for centuries in the Islamic world. Hausa examples may not be true magic squares, but they are believed to be effective in their protective qualities.

KVG

EUROPEAN ART
1200-1945

44

Rinaldo da Siena
Italian (Sienese School), late 13th century
Madonna and Child with Four Saints, ca. 1265-1275
Tempera on wood panel
39 1/2" x 75 1/4" (100.3 cm x 191.1 cm)
Gift of the Samuel H. Kress Foundation 61.210

It is likely that Rinaldo da Siena was a student of Guido da Siena's, founder of the Sienese school, and worked in the master's studio around 1270. The Sienese tradition of painting has its roots in Byzantine art, evidenced in the form and mysticism of the stylized figures. Many common characteristics of Byzantine icons can be found in this work, such as the two-dimensionality of the figures who are depicted with small mouths, long angular noses, and unnaturally elongated fingers. The gold halos surrounding the figures signal their heavenly stature and assist the viewer in seeing them in a dimly lit church.

The gabled dossal, a painting intended to be affixed to an altar, unlike an altarpiece that is hung on the wall, depicts the Madonna and Child flanked by two saints on each side. Early characteristics of Rinaldo's style are evident, including the fleshy chin and large jaw of the male figures and the languid childlike eyes of the female figures. Mary is the largest and most centrally located figure in the composition, signifying her importance to the Sienese and to the religious life of the city. The Christ Child rests in Mary's arms holding a scroll in his left hand, a symbol of his deliverance of the word of God, and gives a gesture of blessing with his right hand. The female saint to the left is Mary Magdalene, identified by the jar of ointment she used to anoint Christ's feet. Margaret of Antioch is represented on the right holding a slender cross, a symbol of Christ's power to heal. The bishop saint on the left is likely to be Saint Sabinus, patron saint of Siena, and the male saint on the right is John the Evangelist, identified by the scroll in his left hand. Angels appear in the arches of the frame, watching over the figures below.

KHD

Lippo di Benivieni
Italian (Florentine School), active 1296-1327
The Crucifixion with Scenes from the Passion and the Life of St. John the Baptist, ca. 1315-1320
Tempera on wood panel
Middle panel, with moldings, 25 1/2" x 13 1/2" (64.8 cm x 34.3 cm)
Left wing, 25 1/2" x 6 7/8" (64.8 cm x 17.5 cm)
Right wing, 24 3/4" x 65 1/2" (62.9 cm x 16.5 cm)
Gift of the Samuel H. Kress Foundation 61.201

A documented member of Florence's art guild, Lippo di Benivieni may have received his early training in Siena. Characterized by the inclusion of elongated figures depicted in rich decorative color and located in a shallow picture plane, 14th-century Sienese painting was typically Medieval in appearance. Lippo's work exhibits an influence of this tradition, as well as that of Florentine master Giotto di Bondone, whose innovative style helped shape the early art of Renaissance Italy. The more naturalistic approach to depicting figures' emotional facial expressions and the manner in which the scenes appear to be illuminated from a single light source are elements inspired by Giotto. Thus, Lippo creates a unique blend of both the Florentine and the Sienese schools of Italian painting.

Made for the personal prayer and devotion of the owner, this small folding triptych was intended to be portable. The central panel depicts the Crucifixion of Christ, rendered in rich color on a gilded background, with the figures displaying the more expressive emotion associated with Florentine painting. Also present in the scene are the Virgin Mary draped in deep blue, John the Baptist with his hand to his cheek, and Mary Magdalene, who mournfully clings to the base of the cross. The human skull depicted behind her, an iconographic reference to Golgotha, locates the scene to the skull-shaped hill where Christ is said to have been crucified. Two Dominican monks, identified by their black-and-gray habits, and an unidentified kneeling woman, wearing a blue-and-gold dress, are also present and may have been included at the request of the patron. The left wing illustrates John the Baptist preaching in the wilderness, his own baptism, and the saint's beheading. The life of Christ is echoed in the opposite wing, portraying Christ praying in the Garden of Gethsemane, the flagellation, and the deposition from the cross.

KHD

48

Spanish (Barcelona)
Processional Cross, ca. 1390
Silver and enamel over an oak core
28 1/2" x 19 7/8" x 1 1/8" (72.4 cm x 50.5 cm x 2.7 cm)
Memphis Brooks Museum of Art Purchase: funds provided by the
Morrie A. Moss Endowment, the Decorative Arts Trust, and Mrs. Lula Coffey 97.9

A processional cross, which played a powerful role in the community, is evidence of the deep religiosity of Medieval life. Housed in a cathedral or church and used in its services, the cross was also employed on important religious and civic occasions. It might have been used in public processions during important feasts such as that of Corpus Christi, or been carried through the city to counter the dreaded effects of plague or natural catastrophes.

Made of sheets of gilded silver on an oak core, the design and decoration of this cross are characteristic of the late Gothic style. The arms, embossed with trailing flower vines, terminate in elegant fleurs-de-lis. Colorful, translucent quatrefoil enamel plaques that picture the Virgin, Saint John, and the symbols of the evangelists are mounted on both sides. On the front an expressive silver gilt figure of the crucified Christ is applied over a red enameled cross. A square plaque of Christ enthroned as judge of the world between two angels appears on the reverse. The surviving enamel and gilding convey a sense of the richness of this sacred object.

This processional cross bears the marks of the silversmiths' guild of Barcelona. Comparison with a nearly identical cross in the Cathedral at Barcelona, stamped and dated 1391, allows the Brooks cross to be dated to the last quarter of the 14th century.

WRB

Taddeo di Bartolo
Italian, ca. 1362-1422
Saint John the Baptist, ca. 1410
Tempera on wood panel
58 1/2" x 17 1/4" (146.6 cm x 43.8 cm)
Gift of the Samuel H. Kress Foundation 61.196

Taddeo di Bartolo
Italian, ca. 1362-1422
Saint James Major, ca. 1410
Tempera on wood panel
57 7/8" x 17 1/2" (147 cm x 43.5 cm)
Gift of the Samuel H. Kress Foundation 61.195

These two narrow panels depicting Saint John the Baptist and Saint James Major were originally part of a polyptych. Companion panels, now in the Kress Collection of the New Orleans Museum of Art, include a Bishop Saint and Saint Catherine of Alexandria. The polyptych probably included a depiction of the Madonna and Child in the central panel, possibly either Taddeo di Bartolo's *Madonna and Child* in the Philbrook Museum or his *Madonna and Child* in the Fogg Museum.[1]

Saint John the Baptist is identified by his hairy fleece tunic and the long reed cross he holds in his left hand. The lettered scroll in front of him reads, in Latin, "Behold the Lamb of God," prophesying the coming of Christ and his sacrifice. Saint James Major holds a decoratively bound book and a pilgrim's staff, and wears a vibrant blue robe under a beautiful red mantle. The brother of Saint John the Evangelist, Saint James Major was an apostle who was tried in Jerusalem in the year 44 and executed by Herod Agrippa.

Taddeo was one of Siena's most important artists, making the Sienese style popular in late-14th-century Italy. As Italy recovered from the ravages of the Black Death, artists like Taddeo enjoyed successful careers painting significant public commissions as part of the reconstruction of urban life. He traveled frequently and his style reflects the many influences encountered during his peripatetic career. The Brooks pictures are characterized by stiff poses and sharp contours, typical of Taddeo di Bartolo's late style.

KF

[1]Gail E. Solberg, *Taddeo di Bartolo: A Polyptych to Reconstruct* (Memphis: Memphis Brooks Museum of Art, 1994), pp. 8-12.

German
Saint Michael, ca. 1450-1480
Limewood, polychromed and gilded
50" x 29" x 16" (127 cm x 73.7 cm x 40.6 cm)
Memphis Brooks Museum of Art Purchase; funds provided by Mr. and Mrs. Ben
B. Carrick, Dr. and Mrs. Marcus W. Orr, Dr. and Mrs. William F. Outlan, Mr. and
Mrs. Downing Pryor, Mr. and Mrs. Richard O. Wilson, Brooks League in memory
of Margaret A. Tate 84.3

Saint Michael the Archangel was a popular subject in late Medieval art. According
to the Book of Revelation (12:7-12), "Michael and his angels fought against the
great dragon . . . that old serpent called the Devil . . . [who] was cast out into the
earth. . . ." By the 5th century a cult had developed around him in his role as the
leader of the heavenly host who defend the Christian Church in its struggle against
evil. In this piece of late Gothic sculpture, Michael is represented as a radiant young
warrior with the two principal attributes symbolizing his role in Medieval
Christendom. He holds in his right hand the upraised sword (the blade is a modern
replacement) as he prepares to strike the dragon. In the left is a remnant of the
scales on which he weighs the souls of the dead at the Last Judgment.

Sculpture was a vital element in Medieval cathedrals, abbeys, and churches, as it
was used to illustrate and reinforce scriptural teaching and church doctrine. This
piece was either part of a large altarpiece or intended to stand alone as a
devotional object. It was carved from limewood, which was commonly used in
Swabia and the Tirol region of southern Germany, and then covered with gesso
and brightly painted, as was most Medieval sculpture. Clad in gilded armor
beneath a red mantle with blue lining, Michael stands on green grass. While much
of the paint has been lost, enough remains to suggest its original striking effect.

The emphasis on detail, characteristic of late Gothic art, is evident in the curls of
the saint's hair, the clasp of his mantle, and the accurate rendering of the complex
armor, down to the buckles, hinges, and lacing. Michael's impassive, stylized facial
expression in the midst of great conflict provides contrast with the sense of motion
suggested by the raised arm, heavy folds of the mantle, and foot draped over the
edge of the grass. These qualities indicate that the piece was carved prior to the
domination of naturalism in German art at the end of the 15th century. The date
can be narrowed further by the dramatically tapering ridged breastplate and
distinctive leg harness with its long, pointed *sabotons* (shoes), which were
fashionable in both armor and clothing between 1430 and 1460.

WRB

German (probably Cologne)
The Mocking of Christ, 1485-1510
Stained glass
28 1/8" x 23 5/8" (71.4 cm x 60 cm)
Gift of the Decorative Arts Trust 99.8

Stained glass, or painted glass as it is more accurately called, was one of the most important art forms in Europe in the late Middle Ages and Renaissance. Windows filled with painted glass provided light and color in cathedrals and churches, and served as important teaching devices, presenting stories from the Bible, the lives of saints, and events in the history of the Church in a graphic way to a largely illiterate population.

The Mocking of Christ almost certainly comes from a series of windows relating the story of the passion of Christ from his entry into Jerusalem to the Resurrection. It recounts the dramatic moment when Christ was handed over by Pilate to soldiers who placed on him a robe and crown of thorns, and mockingly proclaimed, "Hail, King of the Jews." The drama of this event is heightened by the contrast between the cruel, grotesque faces of the soldiers and the idealized, almost serene pathos of the face of Christ, as well as by the use of intense, rich colors.

This panel was made in Germany about 1500, probably for a church in or near Cologne. The subject, spiritual intensity, facial types, and finely detailed drawing of the panel associate it closely with paintings, drawings, and prints of such late-15th- and early-16th-century German masters as Martin Schongauer, Matthias Grünewald, and Albrecht Dürer.

When many churches along the Franco-German border were secularized during the French Revolution, the panel was removed from its original location and taken to England. There it was purchased by Sir William Jernigan, a Roman Catholic, and incorporated along with eighty other panels of early glass into the windows of his private neo-Gothic chapel at Costessey Hall in Norfolk. When the chapel and hall were demolished in the early 20th century, the glass was removed and sold, subsequently finding its way into many public and private collections.

WRB

Albrecht Dürer
German, 1471-1528
The Nativity from *The Small Passion,* 1511
Woodcut
5" x 4" (12.7 cm x 10.2 cm)
Signed: lower right
Gift of the Madonna Circle 60.20.4

Albrecht Dürer was the son of a goldsmith and learned the art of engraving at an early age. He trained in Nuremberg as a goldsmith and painter, and eventually became a prolific printmaker. Dürer's success as a printmaker increased as the use of the printing press expanded greatly during his lifetime, making books and images more widely available and affordable. He produced his first known woodcut at the age of twenty-one and continued to make prints throughout his career, influencing other artists and expanding the popularity of prints. Dürer visited Italy twice and is credited with helping to disseminate Italian Renaissance art in northern Europe.

From the age of twenty-three until his death at fifty-seven, Dürer produced at least six versions of Christ's Passion, the story of Christ's suffering from the Last Supper to the Crucifixion. This depiction of the Nativity was included in the woodcut series *The Small Passion*, published in 1511. Prints were sold on the open market and although commonly printed in groups, series like *The Small Passion* were usually bound together by the owner.

The Nativity is different from other woodcuts in *The Small Passion* series in that the figures are small in scale and the scene is set on a stage above the viewer. The vanishing point of the platform and the stairs is not the same as that of the roof. It is possible that Dürer reworked a design from an earlier series.[1] Dürer's sophisticated mastery of engraving enabled him to emphasize small details, a technique that heightens the viewer's interest in the images. Here, the soles of a shepherd's shoes hang over the edge of the wooden floor, and the tattered remains of thatching are left on the frame of the roof. Through his command of tone, Dürer effected delightful subtleties of light and dark that inspire an emotional response in the viewer. As seen in *The Nativity*, Dürer perfected a technique of close parallel lines and cross-hatchings that suggest light and shadow and gradations of tone.

KF

[1] Erwin Panofsky, *The Life and Art of Albrecht Dürer* (Princeton: Princeton University Press, 1955), p. 140.

Andrea Previtali
Italian (Bergamasque-Venetian School), ca. 1470-1528
The Annunciation, ca. 1520-1525
Tempera on wood panel
61 1/4" x 63 3/8" (155.6 cm x 161 cm)
Gift of the Samuel H. Kress Foundation 61.197

The first record of the painter Andrea Previtali comes from 1502 when he signed and dated one of his paintings and described himself as a disciple of Venetian artist Giovanni Bellini, whose workshop he probably joined between 1490 and 1500. In 1512, Previtali returned to his native Bergamo, where he befriended fellow painter Lorenzo Lotto, and the two became Bergamo's most renowned resident painters. Previtali's use of jewel-like colors, sensuous textures, and soft atmosphere indicate that he never lost his affinity for the works of such Venetian painters as Giovanni Bellini, Titian, and Giorgione.

The Annunciation illustrates the biblical verses Luke 1:28-31, when the Archangel Gabriel announces to the Virgin Mary: "You shall conceive and bear a son, and you shall give him the name Jesus." Gabriel enters Mary's room wearing a jeweled breastplate and carrying a stalk of lilies in his left hand, a symbol of the Virgin's purity. Mary responds to Gabriel's entrance by placing one hand on her breast as she turns away from an open book on the prie-dieu (prayer bench) in front of her. The smoldering candle is a symbol of Christ's incarnation as "the light of the world" and alludes to his Crucifixion. With a gracefully elongated right hand, Gabriel gestures toward the Holy Spirit, appearing in the form of a radiant dove and acting as an intercessor between Mary and Gabriel. The viewer is witness to the dramatic moment of Christ's conception through the Holy Spirit descending from God.

The scene unfolds in a contemporary Italian Renaissance setting, rendered in rich color and charming details, such as the carefully executed basket of fruit on the ledge below the window, the round windowpanes, the ornaments on the coffered ceiling, and the dangling tassels on the canopy above Mary's head.

KHD

Girolamo Romanino
Italian, ca. 1484–after 1560
The Mystic Marriage of Saint Catherine, ca. 1540
Oil on canvas
60 1/4" x 81 3/4" (153 cm x 207.6 cm)
Gift of the Samuel H. Kress Foundation 61.202

In the foreground of the painting the Virgin and Child with Saint Catherine of Alexandria appear in a scene known as _The Mystic Marriage._ Accompanying the main figures are Saint Lawrence, leaning against a marble pillar to the left; Saint Ursula, holding a standard; and Saint Angela Merici, wearing a Franciscan habit and kneeling in prayer on the right. The castle of Brescia can be seen in the background. With the inclusion of Saint Ursula, to whom Angela Merici dedicated her order of Ursulines, and Saint Catherine, this painting most likely commemorates the foundation of the Company of Saint Ursula by Saint Angela Merici on November 25, 1535 (the feast day of Saint Catherine of Alexandria). Saint Lawrence was the namesake of Lorenzo Muzio, the vicar general of Brescia, who approved the Ursuline Order. Angela Merici's death in 1540 probably inspired the commission for Romanino's _The Mystic Marriage of Saint Catherine._

The figures in the painting are dignified and harmoniously arranged, demonstrating an expressionistic realism typical of Romanino's work. The figures appear to interact, creating a strong sense of religious intimacy that makes _The Mystic Marriage of Saint Catherine_ emotionally compelling. The painting's beautiful colors are warm and varied, and the rendering of highlights on the silk drapery is particularly skillful. The detail and rich color of the gowns of Saint Catherine and Mary, the human qualities of the figures, the large scale of the canvas, and the use of soft, aerial perspective are all typically Venetian.

Born in Brescia, Romanino lived his whole life in northern Italy, working in Padua, Mantua, and Brescia, among other cities. He was primarily influenced by the Venetian sensitivity to the effects of color and light, represented principally by Giorgione, Lorenzo Lotto, and Titian. He combined these qualities with elements of Lombard painting, particularly realism, expressiveness, and dramatic intensity. _The Mystic Marriage of Saint Catherine_ is considered one of Romanino's most outstanding works due to its stylistic, historical, and spiritual importance.

KF

Jacopo da Ponte called Jacopo Bassano
Italian, b. ca. 1510-1592
Portrait of a Man of Letters, ca. 1540
Oil on canvas
30" x 25 3/4" (76.2 cm x 65.4 cm)
Signed: lower right
Gift of the Samuel H. Kress Foundation 61.208

Portrait of a Man of Letters is one of Jacopo Bassano's few portraits and the only one that he signed. The subject demonstrates that he is a learned gentleman through the open book that rests under one hand, the adjacent letter, and the glove he holds in the other hand. Balding, dressed in black, and set against an olive-colored background, he seems lost in thought, perhaps pondering something that he has just read. The oriental carpet on the table appears in many of Bassano's paintings and was probably one that he owned and used in his home or studio. The jewel-like colors and the tactile precision with which the color and texture of the carpet are depicted are typical of Bassano's style. The man's position behind the parapet was a somewhat archaic convention at this point in Italian art, but the almost golden light that bathes the sitter is typical of contemporary Venetian painting. Based on his appearance, it is possible that this is a portrait of Giovanni Marcello, a senator and captain in Verona who died in 1555.[1]

Jacopo da Ponte, known as Jacopo Bassano, was apprenticed to his father, also a painter, in the town of Bassano. He trained in Venice and traveled there frequently throughout his life. It is therefore not surprising that Bassano was at first heavily influenced by the Venetian artist Titian. By the middle of the 16th century Bassano's reputation placed him, along with Paolo Veronese and Tintoretto, as one of the most influential northern Italian artists.

KF

[1]W.R. Rearick, "The Portraits of Jacopo Bassano," *Artibus et Historiae*, no.1 (1980): pp. 99-114.

Sofonisba Anguissola
Italian, 1532-1625
Self-Portrait, ca. 1560
Oil on panel
4 1/2" x 4 1/4" (11.4 cm x 10.8 cm)
Memphis Park Commission Purchase 43.11

Sofonisba Anguissola
Italian, 1532-1625
Portrait of One of the Artist's Sisters, ca. 1560
Oil on panel
4 1/2" x 4 5/8" (11.4 cm x 11.7 cm)
Memphis Park Commission Purchase 43.10

Sofonisba Anguissola was born in Cremona and was the most successful in a family of six artist sisters. She was also one of the first female artists to become famous. Anguissola studied at first with Bernardino Campi and later with Bernardino Gatti. In 1559, when she was only twenty-seven, King Philip II of Spain invited her to Madrid, where she worked as a lady-in-waiting and court painter, painting portraits of the royal family and important courtiers. In 1583 she returned to Italy and settled in Palermo.

A prolific painter, Anguissola produced a surprising number of self-portraits. Undoubtedly, this emphasis was due in part to the many restrictions placed on women of the period, who were not allowed to work from nude models. At least twelve self-portraits are known today, ranging from miniature to full-length in size and showing her engaged in a variety of activities, such as reading, painting, and playing instruments. It has not been determined which of Anguissola's five sisters, who often sat for her, is depicted in the second portrait.

Both women stare confidently out at the viewer, making direct eye contact with dignity and in an arresting manner. In her self-portrait, Anguissola wears a bodice with a high neckline and a linen chemise with a stand-up lace collar and delicate tie strings. Cremona was a center of textile production, and in all of her paintings she expertly captures the textures and colors of clothing with great precision. In describing portraits of her family, Giorgio Vasari wrote that they were so lifelike, they seemed to breathe, and it was only their silence that surprised him.

KF

Bartolommeo Manfredi
Italian, 1582-ca. 1621
Ecce Homo, ca. 1612
Oil on canvas
44" x 60" (111.8 cm x 152.4 cm)
Memphis Brooks Museum of Art Purchase 89.12

Emanating from an unseen source on the left, a dramatic and powerful light illuminates four figures, arranged along a narrow ledge, who are seen from below. The men emerge from the blackness, enacting a powerful and dramatic moment in the life of Christ when, according to the gospel, Pontius Pilate offers Christ to the Jewish people. In Bartolommeo Manfredi's *Ecce Homo*, a turbaned Pontius Pilate includes the viewer in the scene with his gesturing right hand and direct eye contact. On the other side of Christ, a helmeted soldier holds up a scarlet-colored garment that encircles Christ's shoulders. The vividness of this blood-red cloak, a symbol of Christ's pending Crucifixion and sacrifice, adds to the visceral impact of the painting. The dramatic intensity created by the crowded figures pushed up close to the viewer and the theatrically lit scene are typical elements of Manfredi's work.

Manfredi is widely recognized as Caravaggio's most important follower because of his ability to imitate the naturalism and chiaroscuro found in Caravaggio's paintings, and it was through his work that many 17th-century Baroque artists interpreted Caravaggio's style. Manfredi's career and life are highly enigmatic due to the lack of documentation about him and his work, and none of his paintings is signed or dated. It was probably after Caravaggio's departure from Rome in 1606 that Manfredi began to build his reputation and attract followers. Although supported by several collectors, Manfredi did not receive large-scale public commissions for churches or other public places. Rather, his paintings were found in the private palaces of Roman and Florentine collectors. The small size of the Brooks painting suggests that it was painted as a private commission.

KF

Jan Lievens
Dutch 1607-1674
Portrait of a Lady in Oriental Dress, ca. 1630
Oil on copper
10" x 8 1/4" (25.4 cm x 21 cm)
Signed: left center
Memphis Brooks Museum of Art Purchase; Morrie A. Moss Acquisition Fund 99.7

Jan Lievens was born in Leiden and by the age of eight was apprenticed to Joris Verschoten. Later, he was sent to Amsterdam to train with Pieter Lastman, who was also the future master of Rembrandt van Rijn (see page 78). By 1625 Lievens was an independent painter with a studio in his father's home, which he might have shared with Rembrandt. After moving to London in 1632, he painted for the court of Charles II. Between 1635 and 1674 he lived primarily in Amsterdam, with time spent also in Antwerp and The Hague. Lievens received several important public commissions during his career, including the town halls of Leiden and Amsterdam and the Huis ten Bosch in The Hague.

The image of a woman in oriental dress is a *tronie* (a bust-length likeness of a specific person not intended to be a portrait) and was probably painted between 1625 and 1630, while Lievens was still living in Leiden. A large middle-aged woman sits in profile, sporting an elaborate oriental or antique costume. It is most likely that her clothes and headdress came from props that Lievens might have kept in his studio. The sitter holds a fan made of the exotic tail feathers from a greater bird of paradise. Since these birds are native to Papua New Guinea, they were extremely rare in Europe at this time and it is interesting to contemplate the source from which Lievens obtained his avian model. The woman is highlighted against a black background by a strong light emanating from an unknown source from the left that beautifully illuminates her plump face, expansive shoulder, and the delicate feathers of her fan. The close, fine painting demonstrated in this *tronie* was typical of the precise brushstrokes and heightened realism found in Lievens' early works.

KF

Roelof Koets
Dutch, 1592-1655
Still Life on a Draped Table, ca. 1635
Oil on panel
29 5/8" x 43" (75.2 cm x 109.2 cm)
Signed: lower left
Memphis Brooks Museum of Art Purchase; Morrie A. Moss Acquisition Fund
2002.2

A table is laid for what appears to be a simple meal, complete with a large glass of wine in a *roemer*, the most popular and inexpensive wineglass used in the 17th century. *Roemers* are easily recognizable by the decorative berry-shaped *prunts* that allowed a glass to be gripped by greasy fingers during meals. Also on display is a herring dripping in butter and capers, an elegant salt cellar, a crisp roll, an ebony-handled knife, and a partially peeled lemon. This light spread rests on a crisply ironed white linen cloth and is embraced by an overturned basket full of grapes, leaves, and vines.

Koets' monochromatic color and painterly execution create a tightly unified image. Unlike earlier Dutch still life traditions, the viewpoint has been brought down lower, almost equal with the viewer. Although it appears straightforward, the painting suggests a complexity of meanings. The inclusion of wine, fish, and bread may have suggested Lenten restraint to 17th-century viewers, and reminded them of the importance of control and abstinence. The expensive and imported goods, however, demonstrate luxury and indulgence. *Still Life on a Draped Table* is both a warning against excess and a demonstration thereof.

Although originally from Zwolle, Koets worked in the tradition of artists from the town of Haarlem, where he lived and worked for most of his career. He was a frequent collaborator with Haarlem still life painter Pieter Claesz. Demonstrations of great technical skill, still lifes demanded an immense specialization and a high level of perfection.

KF

Anthony van Dyck
Flemish, 1599-1641
Portrait of Queen Henrietta Maria, 1638
Oil on canvas
25 1/4" x 19" (64.1 cm x 48.3 cm)
Memphis Park Commission Purchase 43.30

Anthony van Dyck was born in Antwerp and worked briefly in the studio of the famous Flemish artist Peter Paul Rubens, who referred to him as the best of his students. The precocious van Dyck became a court painter to Charles I, who knighted him in 1632. The king recognized van Dyck as the great heir to Titian and commissioned many portraits of himself and of his French queen, Henrietta Maria.

This painting of Henrietta Maria is thought to be one of three portraits commissioned for the Italian sculptor Gianlorenzo Bernini to use in sculpting a portrait bust of the queen. In 1635 Bernini had completed a bust of Charles I (lost in a fire at Whitehall) from a triple portrait by van Dyck. The royal couple was pleased with the result and immediately commissioned a reluctant Bernini to complete a similar bust of the queen.

Two additional painted portrait busts of Henrietta Maria remain in the Royal Collection: a frontal view and a left-facing profile view. The Brooks right-facing profile might have been a third image of this set. The vague shadow of a frontal portrait, however, visible on the right edge of the Brooks canvas, suggests the painting was cut down from its original size and the frontal image painted over. It is therefore possible that the Brooks portrait was not painted at the same time as the two canvases in the Royal Collection. None of the paintings was ever sent to Bernini, presumably due to the political problems facing the English court. In 1642 the English Civil War began and Henrietta Maria fled England for France.

This portrait of Henrietta Maria is one of van Dyck's finest images of the queen. It is exceptional for the relaxed image of the sitter, communicating an almost conversational mood. The soft ringlets that encircle her head seem to echo the opalescent pearls in her hair and around her graceful neck. The beautifully painted satin gown, lace collar, and delicate shawl emphasize the elegance and sensitivity of the queen.

KF

Jan van Bijlert
Dutch, 1597-1671
The Rommel Pot Player, ca. 1639
Oil on canvas
25 3/4" x 19 7/8" (65.4 cm x 50.5 cm)
Memphis Brooks Museum of Art Purchase; Morrie A. Moss Acquisition Fund 96.1

Born in Utrecht, Jan van Bijlert was a pupil first of his father, a glass painter, and then of the painter Abraham Bloemaert. After traveling to France and living in Italy for a short period, Bijlert settled in Utrecht, where he registered as a painter in 1630 and ran an extensive studio. While living in Italy, Bijlert was heavily influenced by Caravaggio and his Italian followers (see page 66). In addition to genre paintings like this one, van Bijlert also painted portraits and history paintings.

Here a young woman in festive attire leans out towards the viewer, emerging out of the surrounding brown background with a fixed stare directed to her left. She is performing with a *rommel pot*, a makeshift drum consisting of a clay pot containing water and covered by a stretched animal bladder that was played with a short stick. A *rommel pot* was often used during popular street festivals and makes frequent appearances in Dutch genre scenes of the period. The exotic plumed turban and fantastic attire of the woman suggest that she is costumed for just such an occasion.

Van Bijlert, along with other Dutch artists such as Hendrick ter Brugghen and Gerrit van Honthorst, was part of the Utrecht Caravaggisti. These artists interpreted Caravaggio's style in a Dutch manner and often with typically Dutch themes, such as *The Rommel Pot Player*. Caravaggesque elements in the Brooks painting, such as the dramatic lighting that illuminates the figure's face and suggestively bare shoulder, and the manner in which the figure projects into the viewer's space, were typical of painting in Utrecht during this period. The woman is startlingly realistic: her hands are dirty and her fingernails, obviously belonging to someone of the working class, are cracked and dirt-encrusted.

KF

Jan van Goyen
Dutch, 1596-1656
River Scene, ca. 1640
Oil on canvas
25 3/8" x 30" (64.5 cm x 76.2 cm)
Gift of Mr. and Mrs. Morrie A. Moss 56.2

Jan van Goyen was born in Leiden and studied in Haarlem with Esaias van de Velde. He was one of the most important and productive landscape painters of 17th-century Holland. Having encountered financial problems after speculating in tulips, van Goyen was an art dealer, collector, auctioneer, estate agent, and appraiser in addition to working as a painter. Extremely prolific, he produced more than 1,200 paintings and over 800 drawings throughout his career.

Although completed in van Goyen's studio, *River Scene* is probably based on drawings made from nature. The painting is marked by tonal unity and a low horizon line, as was common during the 1620s and 1630s. The diagonal line created by the river bluff is typical of van Goyen's work and was a popular technique used to divide the canvas into two segments. As waterways were important for commerce, transportation, irrigation, and shipping, they were frequently depicted in Dutch art. Van Goyen enhances the viewer's interest in the scene by the inclusion of a small boat with two figures inside traveling along the river, probably transporting baskets of produce to or from a market.

Beginning in the 1620s, landscape painting became popular in the Netherlands, and people bought them as enthusiastically as they bought still lifes and genre scenes. A great number of Dutch landscape paintings, like those painted by van Goyen, were produced for the open market. Typically, most emphasize the intimate relationship between humanity and nature through the inclusion of figures: farmers, hunters, herdsmen, and travelers. Here, van Goyen's charming image shows travelers and a soldier in conversation and at rest by a river.

KF

Rembrandt van Rijn
Dutch, 1606-1669
The Omval, 1645
Etching, drypoint, Hind: 210 ii/ii; Holl: 209 ii/ii
7 3/8" x 8 7/8" (18.7 cm x 22.5 cm)
Signed and dated: lower right
Gift of Lois Levy Schwartz 92.1.6

In addition to his skill as a painter, Rembrandt was a master draftsman, and an original and versatile printmaker. He manipulated his burin and copperplate as though they were pencil and paper, developing a unique style different from that of his drawings. *The Omval* is one of twenty-two etchings of diverse subjects by Rembrandt in the Brooks Collection. Even during his lifetime, Rembrandt prints have always been greatly sought after. He had begun etching by 1628, a period when he was still living in Leiden and possibly sharing a studio with Jan Lievens (see page 68).

This etching of the Omval ("the Ruin") possibly resulted from one of Rembrandt's frequent walks in and around Amsterdam. During the 1640s he often depicted his immediate surroundings, although he does not appear to have intended these works to record specific or identifiable locations. Still known by the same name today, the Omval is a small bit of land at the top of a canal that entered the Amstel river south of Amsterdam. A windmill and an arched bridge can be seen on the far right side of the etching, with a covered ferryboat in the middle ground. The scene also includes a second windmill, some moored boats, and a man wearing a broad-rimmed hat with his back to us in the foreground. On closer inspection, an intimate scene of two lovers tucked inside the shadow of the tree on the left can be seen. Rembrandt has created a traditional Italianate scene of pastoral lovers in a typically Dutch setting.

The upper branches of the tree suggest that the print might have been unfinished, a technique common to Rembrandt's etchings. *The Omval* offers a glimpse of one of Rembrandt's earliest uses of drypoint, which became common in his later works. The rich, velvety textures and subtle gradations of tone found in the foreground foliage and tree trunk expertly distinguish the tree and its leaves from the river scene behind. *The Omval*, like Rembrandt's paintings, demonstrates intimacy, drama, and expressive power.

KF

Luca Giordano
Italian, 1634-1705
The Slaying of the Medusa, ca. 1680
Oil on canvas
40" x 135" (101.6 cm x 342:9 cm)
Gift of Mr. and Mrs. Hugo N. Dixon 57.111

Luca Giordano is one of the most important late-17th-century Neapolitan painters. Under the rule of Spain at the time, Naples was the home of many Spanish artists whose bold and dramatic styles influenced his work. Giordano traveled to Rome, Florence, and Venice in his twenties, where his rapid method of painting earned him the nickname "Luca fa presto," or "Luke paints quickly." In 1692 Charles II summoned him to Spain, and Giordano worked there as court painter for ten years. *The Slaying of the Medusa* was probably painted while he was living in Spain.

Giordano was influenced by the illusionistic ceiling paintings of artists such as Pietro da Cortona, which he would have seen while living in Rome. *The Slaying of the Medusa*, and its pendant, *The Massacre of the Children of Niobe*, also in the Brooks Collection, were painted with the image *di sotto in su*, or seen from the bottom upward. Both paintings were probably originally incorporated in an elaborate decorative scheme within a private residence.

The Slaying of the Medusa is a typically exuberant Neapolitan Baroque painting with flowing drapery, frozen dramatic action, and strong colors. Medusa, her head covered with writhing snakes, is lying on a rock next to the two bodies of her monstrous sisters, the immortal Gorgons. Strange feathery wings grow out of the muscular shoulders of the Gorgon on the lower left and her heavy, paw-like hand lies limply in front of her. Perseus, in the center of the canvas and wearing a flowing white cape and red velvet cloak, hefts his sword over his head. In characteristically Baroque fashion, Giordano has captured a tense moment just before Perseus, intently watching his reflection in Athena's shield, lowers the blade and decapitates the recumbent Medusa.

KF

Gaspar Van Wittel or Gaspare Vanvitelli
Dutch, 1652/53-1736
View of the Piazza del Popolo, Rome, ca. 1683
Oil on canvas
28 1/2" x 49 1/2" (72.4 cm x 125.7 cm)
Gift of Mr. and Mrs. Hugo N. Dixon 54.4

Gaspar Van Wittel was born in Utrecht and moved to Italy in 1674, where he became known by the Italian version of his name, Gaspare Vanvitelli. He lived most of his life in Rome and became famous for his *vedute* (views) of Rome and other Italian cities. Visitors to Rome on the Grand Tour during the 18th century sought souvenirs of their trips, creating a market for *vedute* like the *View of the Piazza del Popolo*. Vanvitelli painted this popular scene on at least five other occasions.

Most visitors from the north arriving in Rome in the 17th or 18th century entered the city through the Porta del Popolo. From this gate they gained their first view of Rome and the Piazza del Popolo, one of the city's finest squares. Perhaps Vanvitelli initially sketched the piazza from the top of the gate, thereby offering the viewer an expansive picture of the city of Rome lying beyond the Piazza del Popolo. In the distance the Villa Medici, the Quirinal Palace, the dome of the Pantheon, and the cupola of Sant'Andrea della Valle can be seen. In the center of the square sits the ancient Egyptian obelisk originally erected in the Circus Maximus by Augustus in 10 B.C.E. and moved to this square in 1589. The parish church of Santa Maria del Popolo is just visible to the left. At the southern end of the square are the 17th-century twin churches Santa Maria dei Miracoli and Santa Maria di Montesanto.

The shadows stretching out to the right indicate that this scene takes place in the serene light of the early morning. Vanvitelli is famous for the soft, harmonious colors and subtle atmosphere seen here. Charming details of life in the city have been captured: smoke rising from a chimney, laundry hanging from an open window, flaking paint covering ancient walls, and the beggars, dandies, prelates, and tradesmen who move about the city.

KF

Sebastiano Ricci
Italian, 1659-1734
The Finding of Moses, ca. 1710
Oil on canvas
51 7/8" x 42" (131.8 cm x 106.7 cm)
Gift of the Samuel H. Kress Foundation 61.204

Sebastiano Ricci was born in the provincial town of Belluno to a family of artists. After receiving his training in Venice, he traveled widely and worked in London, Vienna, Bologna, Turin, and Paris. Ricci's style developed under the influence of Venetian painter Paolo Veronese, and Ricci's paintings are sometimes mistaken for works by Veronese. Often in trouble with the authorities over his amorous exploits and dangerous lifestyle, Ricci's frequent scandals appear to have had little impact on his success as an artist.

The Finding of Moses is probably a pendant to *Jephthah and His Daughter*, also in the Brooks Kress Collection. The paintings were made around 1710 and demonstrate the influence that Veronese's style exerted on Ricci's work. His typically painterly style and luminous palette can be seen in the elaborate dresses and deep skin tones of the pharaoh's daughter's attendants. The artist developed a tight composition and the figures crowd the canvas with a taut circular unity. With his light, elegant style, rich colors, and playful compositions, Ricci is often seen as one of the founders of the Rococo style.

The story of *The Finding of Moses* is included in Exodus 2:9, when Pharaoh's daughter said to the woman: "Take this child and nurse it for me, and I will pay you your wages." Ricci returned to the subject of the finding of Moses on several occasions. The fair coloring of the pharaoh's daughter and the figures' 18th-century clothes indicate that the artist did not seek historical accuracy.

KF

George Tyler
English (London), apprenticed 1689-last known work 1735
Longcase Clock, ca. 1710-1720
Walnut with arabesque marquetry in holly and other woods; oak; brass
100 3/4" x 20 1/2" x 9" (255.9 cm x 52.1 cm x 22.9 cm)
Gift of Brooks Art Gallery League, Inc. 82.10

The pendulum clock, developed about 1657 in the Netherlands by Christian Huygens, revolutionized timekeeping by reducing the margin of error from fifteen minutes to a few seconds per day. It was soon adopted in England, where it reached its apogee; the clock movements made there between 1680 and 1720 are considered the finest of the day.

George Tyler made the eight-day movement with anchor escapement of this clock during that golden age. He was apprenticed in 1692 through the Worshipful Company of Clockmakers to the well-known London maker Robert Dingley. After gaining his freedom in 1699, Tyler maintained his own shop in Pope's Head Alley, London, until his death.

Leading cabinetmakers of the day created elaborately decorated cases that were designed to conceal and protect the unsightly pendulum and lead weights. From about 1700 until 1720, fashion dictated great height in these luxury furnishings. The allover arabesque marquetry decoration on the front of the case is typical of the most sophisticated English work of the period, with symmetrically arranged floral designs in contrasting light and dark woods. This elaborate decorative work followed designs published in France by Jean Berain, and popularized by the brass and tortoiseshell furniture decoration of André-Charles Boulle, the leading French cabinetmaker of the reign of Louis XIV.

WRB

English
Young Boy's Waistcoat, ca. 1720
Linen with silk embroidered appliqués
Back length: 20 1/4" (51.4 cm)
Gift of the Decorative Arts Trust 95.2

In the early 18th century, one of the principal influences upon design in England continued to be the Far East. It had affected nearly every branch of craftsmanship in the country since the mid-17th century, when commercial trade with the East increased. The vogue for oriental wares, chinoiserie, was reflected in the many fabric patterns that decorated household furnishings as well as personal dress. Embroidered goods incorporated many Anglicized Indian and Chinese motifs, such as pagodas, bridges, dragons, or, more commonly, the exotic flowers, birds, and butterflies that adorn this small child's waistcoat.

The front of this garment is covered in a whimsical design composed of embroidered appliqués placed in a symmetrical pattern. Each motif—rendered in vibrant hues of yellow green, bright pink, rich blue, or mustard yellow—contains several rows of graduated color that replicates shading on the leaves, petals, and feathers, and provides a lively contrast. Worked in a chain stitch with French knot accents, these appliqués were produced with fine silk thread on a separate piece of linen, cut to shape, and then sewn onto the coat. This practice was less time consuming than embroidering directly on the ground fabric, as more than one worker could assist in the production of a garment. In professional shops, this technique helped keep production costs down. Another advantage was that appliqués could be removed easily and later reapplied to another ground fabric.

This waistcoat is made of simple linen, but more elaborate ones were sewn in silk fabrics and included embroidery with gold and silver metallic threads. Expensive fashionable waistcoats continued to be embroidered up until the second half of the 19th century.

MM

Giovanni Antonio Canal, called Canaletto
Italian, 1697-1768
The Grand Canal from Campo di San Vio, 1730-1735
Oil on canvas
44 3/8" x 63 3/8" (112.7 cm x 161 cm)
Gift of the Samuel H. Kress Foundation 61.216

Giovanni Antonio Canal, known as Canaletto, was born in Venice and worked for his father, a successful theatrical scene painter. In 1719 Canaletto traveled to Rome where he probably encountered the work of other artists painting *vedute* (views), such as Gaspare Vanvitelli (see page 82). Shortly after his return to Venice in 1720 Canaletto began depicting scenic views of the city. His paintings were primarily collected by Englishmen on the Grand Tour, which was an important part of the education and maturation of wealthy young Englishmen. *Vedute*, such as Canaletto's *The Grand Canal*, served as souvenirs as well as visible proof of the impressive journey.

The Grand Canal from Campo di San Vio was painted for the Englishman George Proctor. Its pendant, also a gift of the Samuel H. Kress Foundation, *The Molo: Looking West, Ducal Palace Right*, is in the collection of the El Paso Museum of Art. The subject of the canal seen from the Campo di San Vio was one of Canaletto's favorite images of Venice and at least twelve versions of this scene, painted in the 1720s and 1730s, are known today. In each of these paintings Canaletto selected a slightly different viewpoint or included a varied assemblage of boats and people.

Here the viewer looks east along the Grand Canal, with the peeling façade of the Palazzo Barbarigo in the foreground and a woman leaning out of the upper balcony. The perspective on the south side of the canal terminates at the Punta della Dogana and includes the dome of Santa Maria della Salute above the palaces at the right. One of the most majestic palaces on the Grand Canal, the Palazzo Corner della Ca' Grande, designed by Jacopo Sansovino, perches on the north side. The viewer's first reaction to Canaletto's paintings is often to believe that they offer a descriptive representation of what the artist actually saw. His work, however, involves extensive manipulation of buildings, piazzas, canals, and perspective. Paintings such as *The Grand Canal* show the influence of Canaletto's earlier work as a scene painter for the theater, demonstrated by the ease with which he captures interesting lighting and multiple viewpoints. Canaletto's fascination with people is evidenced by the beggars, gondoliers, tradesmen, and aristocrats who populate his *vedute* paintings.

KF

Thomas Heming
English (London), active ca. 1745-at least 1782
Tea Canister and Sugar Canister in Shagreen Box, 1753
Silver, wood, shagreen
Box: 7 5/8" x 7 3/8" x 4 7/8" (19.4 cm x 18.8 cm x 12.7 cm)
Canister b: 5 3/8" x 4" x 3 1/8" (13.7 cm x 10.2 cm x 8 cm)
Canister c: 5 1/8" x 4" x 2 5/8" (13.1 cm x 10.2 cm x 6.7 cm)
Gift of the Decorative Arts Trust 2002.1a.b.c.

Tea, introduced into Europe from the Far East and originally valued for its medicinal qualities, became a regular part of the English diet by the early 18th century. An important ritual in fashionable circles, afternoon tea called for specialized equipment: tea table, hot water urn, teapot, cups and saucers, and spoons. Canisters were developed to hold the tea leaves and sugar. Since the service of tea was a formal, even ceremonial event, this equipment was usually decorative as well as utilitarian.

This set of silver tea and sugar canisters was made in 1753 in London by Thomas Heming, Principal Goldsmith to the King (George III) from 1760 until 1782, in the Rococo chinoiserie style that was the height of fashion. On front and back, a romanticized Chinese tea picker, harvesting the tea and placing it in a wickerwork basket, is framed in an elaborate Rococo cartouche composed of asymmetrical scrolls, shells, and lion masks. On each side a stylized Asian thatched house stands beneath a palm tree. The chinoiserie motifs suggest the exotic Chinese origin of the tea served in England, and the Rococo elements convey a sense of the elegant fantasy characteristic of mid-18th-century aristocratic society.

Because tea was an expensive imported commodity subject to a high government duty, it was often stored under lock and key. These silver canisters are housed in their original fitted box covered with shagreen—a rough, untanned leather from the hide of a shark, seal, or horse—and mounted with silver Rococo escutcheons and handle. The box is supported on silver ball-and-claw feet similar to those on furniture in the Chippendale style of the 1750s and 1760s.

WRB

Richard Wilson
English, b. ca. 1713-1782
Tivoli: Temple of the Sibyl and the Campagna, ca. 1763-1767
Oil on canvas
37" x 49 1/2" (94 cm x 125.7 cm)
Gift of Mr. and Mrs. Morrie A. Moss 59.26

Perched on a hilltop to the left stand the ruins of the Temple of the Sibyl, surrounded by the modern town of Tivoli. In the foreground, sitting below a curved tree are two figures: an artist sketching while another man, probably a peasant, leans on a stick and looks over the artist's shoulder. The arch of the peasant's back perfectly echoes that of the spindly tree opposite him. The wide plain of the Campagna stretches out to the horizon, offering a vista all the way to Rome. This Arcadian view of the countryside, complete with crumbling ruins, was intended to inspire thoughts of idyllic beauty and human transience. With the onset of the Industrial Revolution, many British aristocrats fulfilled a nostalgia for a more bucolic past through paintings like Richard Wilson's image of Tivoli.

Tivoli was a popular destination for 18th-century travelers, especially poets, artists, and authors. It was associated with the ancient pastoral poetry of Theocritus, Virgil, and Horace. This view was probably based on drawings Wilson made in his sketchbooks while living in Italy, but painted later in his British studio. Wilson frequently produced multiple versions of his best-selling paintings and several other versions of this scene exist.

Although he started his career as a portrait painter, Wilson was one of the first important British landscape painters. Born in Wales, he traveled to Italy in 1750, where he encountered Italian and French landscape painters working in the romanticized tradition of Claude Lorrain and Gerard Dughet. After his return to Britain in 1756 or 1757, Wilson specialized in idealized landscapes of Italy and paintings of country manor houses for the aristocracy. Although he was a founding member of the Royal Academy, Wilson never achieved great acclaim during his lifetime, and by 1770, suffering ill health, his career had foundered.

KF

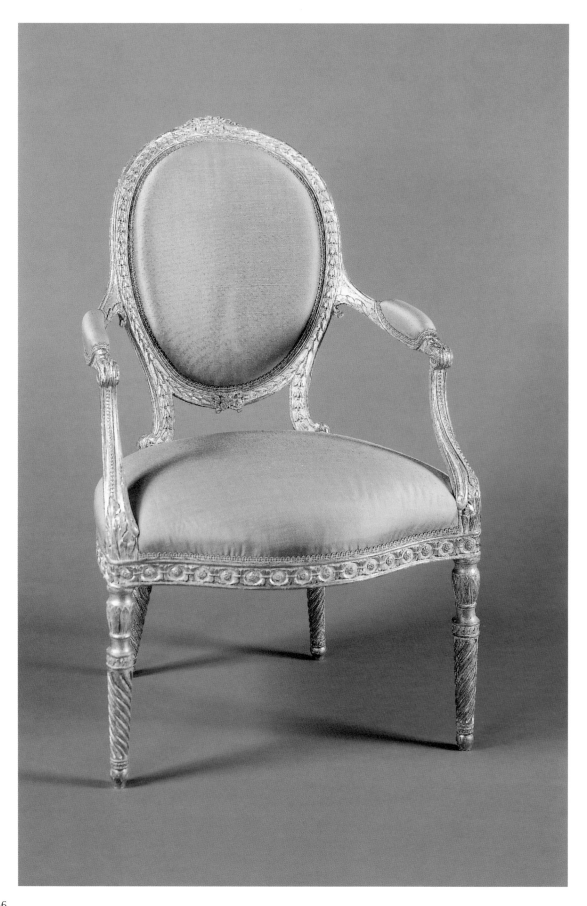

English
Armchair, ca. 1770-1780
Giltwood (probably beech), silk
38 1/2" x 24" x 20 3/4" (97.8 cm x 63.5 cm x 52.7 cm)
Memphis Brooks Museum of Art Purchase; funds provided through exchange by
Maud Mason 83.14

Robert Adam, the Scottish architect-designer, returned in 1758 from three years in Italy greatly influenced by the classical art of ancient Rome and the Renaissance. He established a practice in London and became the most important advocate of the Neoclassical style in Britain. Best known for his work on the interiors of the houses of great aristocratic clients, Adam designed not only the decoration of the ceilings and walls, but also the carpets, furniture, and silver. As a result of his work and that of contemporaries such as the cabinetmakers John Linnell and Matthias Lock, Neoclassicism supplanted the Rococo in English furniture design and decoration, and remained dominant until the end of the 18th century. There was a new emphasis on symmetry, restraint, a controlled blending of straight and curved lines, and decorative motifs drawn from antiquity.

In 1777, Adam designed a set of armchairs for the state bedchamber of Osterley Park, near London, one of his most important commissions. These are described in the inventory of 1782 as "richly Carved and gilt in burnish Gold covered with green Velvet flannel. . . ."[1] This giltwood armchair is a somewhat simplified version of his design for that set. Its relatively small size, oval concave back, molded frame, and straight tapering legs are dramatic departures from the playful, asymmetrical, curvilinear Rococo tradition, while the gracefully sloping arm supports, serpentine seat rails, and spiral turning of the legs reveal its persistence. Neoclassical emphasis on balance and grace and the Greco-Roman influence are especially evident in the carved decoration—*paterae*, tied bows, acanthus, and bellflowers. The gilded surface, often found on early Neoclassical English chairs, enhances the elegance and lightness of this piece, and provides a striking contrast with the somber walnut and mahogany surfaces previously popular.

WRB

[1]Maurice Tomlin, *Catalogue of Adam Period Furniture* (London: Victoria and Albert Museum, 1982), pp. 66-67.

Thomas Gainsborough
English, 1727-1788
Gainsborough Dupont, ca. 1775-1776
Oil on canvas
30" x 24 7/8" (76.2 cm x 63.2 cm)
Gift of Mr. and Mrs. Morrie A. Moss 61.173

Thomas Gainsborough was born in Suffolk and began to study as a silversmith at the age of thirteen. However, he never had any formal academic training as a painter. An original founder of the Royal Academy in 1768, he exhibited in the first exhibition of the Royal Academy in 1769. By the end of his career, Gainsborough was a great rival of the painter Sir Joshua Reynolds, whose work can also be seen in the Brooks Collection.

Gainsborough Dupont was Thomas Gainsborough's nephew and, from 1772, was also his uncle's assistant, the only one that he appears to have employed. Apparently hoping that Dupont would carry on his legacy, at his death Gainsborough left Dupont one hundred pounds and all of his paints, varnishes, tools, models, and painting utensils. In 1775, at the age of seventeen, Dupont entered the Royal Academy School; it was at about this time that his uncle painted the Brooks' portrait of him. Probably because he was kept busy working in his uncle's studio, Dupont did not exhibit at the Royal Academy until 1790, two years after his uncle's death. Dupont went on to have moderate success as a portrait painter, but died at the young age of forty-two.

Gainsborough drew or painted his nephew on several occasions. Here he can be seen—a bright and slender young man of about twenty years of age—painted in a dignifying oval, looking out to the right with his gaze fixed firmly on the viewer. As was highly fashionable at the time, his hair is dressed and powdered. The Brooks' portrait is very similar to the final self-portrait that Gainsborough painted around 1787 and is now in the collection of the Royal Academy in London.

KF

George Romney
English, 1734-1802
Portrait of Lady Wright, 1779-1780
Oil on canvas
30 1/4" x 25" (76.8 cm x 63.5 cm)
Gift of Mr. and Mrs. Morrie A. Moss 59.47

Lady Wright was the wife of Sir Sampson Wright, chief magistrate of Bow Street. In her portrait she sits in an elevated and angled position with her eyes firmly fixed on the viewer just below her. During the 1780s, George Romney frequently painted his female sitters in wide-brimmed hats, as can be seen here where Lady Wright wears a large cream-colored hat with a very wide brim and pale ribbon. Lady Wright's dress is a rich mauve taffeta with ruffles around the neck and sleeves. The seriousness of her expression is contrasted by the frivolous feathery exuberance of the lace and ribbons on her hat and clothes. The immediacy of Romney's brushstrokes gives the impression that the painting was dashed off quickly, a quality for which Romney was famous. As recorded in his sitter books, however, Lady Wright sat for Romney on seven occasions between 1779 and 1780.

Romney left school around the age of ten to work with his father, a cabinetmaker; apprenticed to a painter in 1755; and then started his own practice. In 1773 he closed his shop and moved to Rome. Although he had to borrow money in order to return to London in 1775, shortly after reestablishing his practice he quickly became the most fashionable portrait painter in London. His prices were set lower than those of Sir Joshua Reynolds (represented in the Brooks Collection) and Thomas Gainsborough (see page 98), perhaps a gesture made to distinguish himself in the market from his contemporary rivals. Apparently afraid of criticism, Romney refused to show his work at the Royal Academy. It was appealing to many of his clients that their privacy would be protected and their portraits would not hang in public exhibition spaces. After Romney's death, however, the *Portrait of Lady Wright* was eventually displayed in the Royal Academy's winter exhibition of 1887.

KF

Sir Henry Raeburn
Scottish, 1756-1823
Portrait of Charles Gordon, Fourth Earl of Aboyne, ca. 1785
Oil on canvas
50 1/4" x 40" (127.6 cm x 101.6 cm)
Memphis Park Commission Purchase 43.16

Looking relaxed and thoughtful, Charles Gordon is seated in a green leather chair near an open window. Wearing a fashionable wig, Gordon is sporting a brown coat, white vest, and black breeches, all depicted in complementary hues. A rich green velvet drapery has been pulled back to reveal a wooded landscape outside of the window, very likely Gordon's estate. Gordon's education and intelligence are emphasized by the books, inkwell, letters, and envelope placed on the table to his left. The soft light that falls through the open window illuminates the painting's rich colors and subtle hues. Gordon's contemplative and poetic mood creates a quiet atmosphere of intimacy.

In 1778 Gordon raised the Gordon Highlanders of Fencibles and his son, the Marquis of Huntley, raised the independent Black Watch. His wife, Lady Jane Maxwell, introduced the tartan plaids of these companies. A soldier and statesman, Gordon traveled frequently.

Sir Henry Raeburn, who was born in Scotland and orphaned at a young age, received early training as a goldsmith, but was largely self-taught as a portrait painter. In London he met Sir Joshua Reynolds (represented in the Brooks Collection), who had a significant influence on his work. No drawings or preliminary studies exist for Raeburn's portraits, and he appears to have worked quickly and directly on the canvas. Establishing his practice in Edinburgh by 1787, Raeburn became the primary Scottish portrait painter of the period. He was knighted in 1822 when King George IV visited Edinburgh.

KF

Attributed to Thomas Harley
English, active ca. 1805-1824
Advertising Jug, ca. 1805-1808
Earthenware
12 1/2" x 15 1/2" (31.8 cm x 39.4 cm)
Gift of Mary Semmes Orr in honor of Stella Stroh Menke 91.7

Metallic lustreware was developed in Staffordshire in northern England around 1800 to provide an inexpensive imitation of the silver and porcelain used by the upper classes. It was created by applying a thin coating of metal oxide to an earthenware object that was then fired to produce a lustrous surface. When platinum was used, the piece would resemble silver; when gold was applied, various hues—such as gold, copper, lavender, or pink—would result, according to the amount of metal used in the solution and the color of the clay body. Lustreware could be decorated with transfer prints or stenciling, or painted freehand with colored enamels. It was very popular and was produced in great quantity in potteries throughout northern England and Wales until replaced around 1850 by the newly developed, inexpensive electroplated silver.

Probably the most popular lustreware form was the jug used for milk or other liquids, which could be purchased in a wide range of sizes. This unusually large jug (part of the Brooks' large collection of 19th-century English lustreware) was not intended for domestic use. Instead, it was created for display in a shop window to attract attention to the types of wares sold, thereby earning the popular name "advertising jug." The form and decoration of this jug are characteristic of the work of Thomas Harley, a well-known potter who produced lustreware in his own workshop in Lane End, Longton, Staffordshire, between 1805 and 1808, and then in partnership as Harley and Seckerson Company until 1824. Relief-molded, the jug's raised diamond-shaped decoration resembles the surface of a pineapple. The body of the piece is soft yellow with alternating diamonds in brightly contrasting silver lustre. This motif is sometimes called the harlequin pattern because of its similarity to the diamond-shaped design decorating the clothing of Harlequin, the well-known character from the Italian *commedia dell'arte* and model for the jack-in-the-box.

WRB

Cléambault
French (Alençon)
Bed Curtains (part of a five piece *garniture de lit*), completed in 1809
Linen, needle lace
144" x 98" (each panel) (365.8 cm x 248.9 cm)
Gift of Warner S. McCall in memory of his wife, Jennie Owen McCall (1876-1946)
50.16a-b

The lace-making industry was established in France through a 1665 proclamation by Louis XIV. By the time Napoleon came to power in the early 19th century, the French lace industry was near collapse. Recent political upheavals had caused the disruption of international trade and many trained lace makers had fled the country. To encourage the industry's return to prosperity, Napoleon made the wearing of Alençon and Argentan lace compulsory at court. During this period he also commissioned a number of important lace items from French workshops, including a lavish set of lace bed furnishings for Empress Josephine. This order called for one of the largest pieces of Alençon lace ever produced, requiring an extraordinary number of workers and man-hours. Because it took nearly ten years to complete, the *garniture de lit* was subsequently presented to the Archduchess Marie-Louise at the time of her marriage to Napoleon rather than to Josephine.

The order for the exquisite five-piece set was placed with M. Deshaleries of Paris and produced by the firm of Cléambault. The set's intricate and regal design reflects Empress Josephine's extravagant taste. The bed curtains include the imperial bee in a diaper pattern powdered across the ground (*réseau ordinaire*) with Napoleonic crowns in all four corners. Along the border are delicate imperial lilies, and on the very edge is an Empire pattern of berries repeated with a band of fine fillings (*modes*). The exceptional effects of light and shade are achieved through variations of the buttonhole stitch. The clear and sharply defined quality of the design is characteristic of needle lace, and *point d'Alençon* was considered one of the finest and most aristocratic.

Additional pieces that complete the set are included in the following collections: sections of the valance, the Brooklyn Museum and the Cooper-Hewitt Museum; bed coverlet, the Rhode Island School of Design; and canopy, the Toledo Museum. The original bed for which they were created is in the Napoleonic Museum, Malmaison.

MM

Jules Dupré
French, 1811-1889
Pastoral Scene, 1870
Oil on canvas
23 5/8" x 27 3/4" (60 cm. x 70.5 cm)
Signed and dated: lower right
Gift of Mr. and Mrs. Morrie A. Moss 59.29

Jules Dupré was one of the principal members of the Barbizon school, which changed the traditional concept of landscape painting in France in the 19th century. Soon after Dupré left his work as a porcelain painter in 1829, he joined with artists such as Théodore Rousseau, Jean-Baptiste-Camille Corot (represented in the Brooks Collection), and Charles-François Daubigny painting *en plein air* (out of doors) in the forests of Fountainebleau in the 1830s and 1840s. Initially trained as an industrial artist, Dupré took study trips to Paris and Great Britain to help develop his innate talent. His work was heavily influenced by 17th-century Dutch landscapes and their direct and realistic observation of nature and humanity. These qualities were also evident in the innovative work of British painter John Constable, whom Dupré studied intently while in London. This same direct approach was adopted by the Barbizon painters in response to the idealized and classically composed landscapes preferred by the French Academy.

Over the course of his career, Dupré's work ranged from dramatic seascapes to quietly romantic rural scenes with cottages, cattle, or winding streams. *Pastoral Scene* was painted during the latter part of his life when the artist resided at L'Isle-Adam, north of Paris, and spent his summers along the coast at Cayeux sur Mer. With its low horizon line, towering silhouetted tree, and enormous expanse of cloud-dappled sky that dwarfs the figures and animals, this work is reminiscent of earlier Dutch compositions. Although Dupré employed free and direct brushwork in many of his paintings, the handling of paint in this canvas is more conservative. His small precise strokes denote every leaf on the tree and render minute details in the foreground brush. The sky, which is more loosely applied, sets the atmosphere of the scene and conveys distinct weather conditions in the manner of Constable. In its depiction of the untouched countryside, this picture also reflects a spiritual regard for nature that characterized the work of the Barbizon painters.

MM

Alfred Sisley
French, 1839-1899
Le Pont d'Argenteuil (The Bridge at Argenteuil), 1872
Oil on canvas
15 1/4" x 24" (38.7 cm. x 61 cm)
Signed and dated: lower right
Gift of Mr. and Mrs. Hugo N. Dixon 54.64

Born in Paris, Alfred Sisley studied in the studio of Marc Charles-Gabriel Gleyre from 1860 to 1864 with fellow students Claude Monet, Pierre-Auguste Renoir, and Jean-Frédéric Bazille. Gleyre's approach encouraged working with a palette specifically prepared to accommodate painting quickly *en plein air* (out of doors). Sisley and his classmates later employed these methods when they became interested in recording their visual perceptions of nature and the transitory effects of light and weather. These overriding concerns led to the evolution of what critics eventually called Impressionism. By 1874, when Sisley participated in the *First Impressionist Exhibition*, he had adopted a bold, broken brushstroke and a brighter color palette, like his colleagues. But unlike Monet and Renoir, who included figures in their work, Sisley remained dedicated, almost exclusively, to painting the landscape throughout his career.

While living in Louveciennes in 1872, Sisley visited Monet at Argenteuil and produced a series of paintings of the town and its environs. *Le Pont d'Argenteuil* depicts the road bridge crossing the Seine with Petit Gennevilliers on the right and Argenteuil on the left. Sisley's carefully balanced composition includes a pathway directing the viewer's gaze to a horizon line formed by a distant railway bridge and the hills of Sannois. In this idyllic scene, puffs of clouds dot the sky above as a sailboat floats on the water and a boatman walks from the shore, bent under the weight of his oars. With small, swift strokes of raw sienna, green, and salmon set against the gray blue expanse of water and sky, Sisley captures the fleeting atmosphere of a softly lit wintry day along the Seine. Édouard Manet, who owned the painting, lent it for inclusion in the *Third Impressionist Exhibition* of 1877.

MM

Camille Pissarro
French, 1831-1903
La Sente de Justice, Pontoise (Justice Path at Pontoise), ca. 1872
Oil on canvas
20 5/8" x 32 1/8" (52.4 cm x 81.6 cm)
Signed: lower left
Gift of Mr. and Mrs. Hugo N. Dixon 53.60

Artists of the Impressionist movement, which began in France in the late 19th century, typically painted landscapes and scenes of modern life. Through the use of pure colors and loose brushstrokes, they demonstrated the momentary effects of light, atmosphere, and movement. Camille Pissarro, one of the first Impressionist painters, grew up on the island of St. Thomas in the French West Indies. In 1855 he moved to Paris, where he studied only briefly at the École des Beaux-Arts because he disliked the inflexible and rigid approach of the school. Eventually Pissarro sought instruction outside the classroom and was greatly influenced by Jean-Baptiste-Camille Corot (represented in the Brooks Collection), who taught him to seek beauty in modest landscapes. He followed Corot's dictum of painting *en plein air* (out of doors), depicting one's visual experiences, and rendering the effects of light and climate. Like many of his contemporaries, Pissarro left Paris for the countryside in 1855.

From 1866 to 1882 the painter lived and worked in Pontoise, a small town outside of Paris. Away from the city, he experimented painting *en plein air*, creating some of his best-known works—serene scenes, like this one, where the true subject is the impression of the time of day or the season. Using flat planes of color and the effects of light, he defined the volume of the buildings and, through comma-like brushstrokes, created the richly textured leaves and grasses. This painting is characterized by a light palette that the artist used from 1870 until 1880, including the yellow greens in the foliage and vegetation, the pale blue of the sky, the gray of the buildings and smoke, and the buff and beige of the soil, the tree trunks, and the path. An implied arc, the walking trail leads the viewer's eye to the two strolling figures and then around to the cityscape. In portraying the extensive site of Pontoise, Pissarro contrasts the open natural environment of the countryside with the town's solid mass of geometric buildings and industrial smokestacks. Through this juxtaposition, the artist alludes to the encroaching Industrial Revolution and the dramatic changes it made on the French landscape.

KVG

William-Adolphe Bouguereau
French, 1825-1905
Au Pied de la Falaise (At the Foot of the Cliff), 1886
Oil on canvas
43 1/4" x 26 1/4" (109.9 cm. x 66.7 cm)
Signed and dated: lower left
Gift of Mr. Morrie A. Moss 93.4

In the last half of the 19th century, as the French art world was undergoing dynamic changes with the advent of Impressionism, William-Adolphe Bouguereau remained committed to traditional painting methods and aesthetics. After receiving his training at the École des Beaux Arts in Paris, he followed Michelangelo and Raphael in using the human figure as a means of expression. He was an exceptional draftsman, and his early canvases of historical, mythological, and biblical scenes consisted of highly finished figures set in classical compositions. These subjects brought him commissions from churches, government institutions, and private residences. When he later began to produce paintings of female peasants, mothers, and children, which had greater appeal in the public marketplace, his financial success was secured. Although he also accrued many state honors and international awards, and held prestigious positions in the Parisian art world, critics often condemned his work for being too sentimental and executed with an almost mechanical accuracy.

This painting of a seated young girl displays Bouguereau's mastery of the human body and his unsurpassed ability to replicate textures. Typical of his work, the child is nearly life-size, sitting in a natural relaxed pose with eyes gazing to the left in a wistful or contemplative manner. Although he painted his peasant subjects with realistic precision, Bouguereau idealized them with flawless skin, spotless clothes, and perfect proportions. He saw art as a highly selective process whereby the artist improved on reality to create an image that was poetic and universal. Many of his peers viewed his work as empty perfection, but Bouguereau, whose passion for the figure was inexhaustible, continued painting in this style until his death in 1905.

MM

Édouard Vuillard
French, 1868-1940
Vue en Suisse (View in Switzerland), 1900
Oil on wood panel
16" x 32 1/4" (40.6 cm x 81.9 cm)
Signed: lower left
Gift of Mr. and Mrs. Hugo N. Dixon 55.48

Édouard Vuillard was born in Cuiseaux, France. After the death of his father, his mother moved to Paris to work as a dressmaker. As Vuillard's grandfather and uncle were textile designers, he grew up surrounded by designs, patterns, and textures. He attended the École des Beaux-Arts and the Académie Julian, where he met Pierre Bonnard and Maurice Denis. They formed the group called the Nabis, a name derived from the Hebrew word for prophet, and sought inspiration from 19th-century Japanese woodcuts and French Symbolist paintings. Their primary influence, however, was Paul Gauguin's bold two-dimensional style and his belief that the expression of ideas, mood, and emotion were more important than naturalistic representation. Their works are characterized by the emotional or decorative use of flat color patterns and linear distortion. Like the other Nabis, Vuillard primarily painted interior scenes using a muted palette to create works of subtle texture and pattern. His paintings are complex tapestries of quiet, cultivated middle-class life.

In the early years of the 20th century Vuillard began to show his work at Bernheim-Jeune, a Parisian gallery, and was encouraged by his dealers to explore other subjects. A sojourn in Switzerland sparked a new awareness of the countryside and inspired him to paint landscapes. Often enclosed by trees or vegetation, his landscapes have an intimate quality, much like indoor spaces. *Vue en Suisse* depicts a summer day with lush fruit trees ripening under blue skies and a lone figure standing amid a sheltered grove. Although naturalistic, Vuillard has simplified the principal elements, depicting the orchards in flat areas of color with loosely rendered details. The outlines of the trees, branches, and foliage form abstract patterns, while his brushstrokes create a subtle textile-like design of mottled grass and trees. Using pale light and areas of neutral colors, Vuillard evokes a mood of restful calm, similar to that of his interior scenes.

KVG

Maurice Utrillo
French, 1883-1955
Vue de Sannois (View of Sannois), 1912
Oil on canvas
13 3/8" x 16 1/2" (33.9 cm x 41.9 cm)
Signed: lower right
Bequest of Julie Isenberg 87.20.7

Maurice Valadon was the illegitimate son of painter Suzanne Valadon; his father, Miguel Utrillo, did not admit paternity until eight years after Maurice's birth. By the age of twelve, the child was a regular patron of the cafés in Montmartre; by thirteen, he was an alcoholic, and he eventually became a drug addict. With his increased use of absinthe came signs of mental degeneration, and he was confined to an asylum at the age of eighteen. Utrillo was advised to take up art as a form of occupational therapy while institutionalized in 1902.

At nineteen, seeking subject matter for his art and refuge from city life, he moved to the countryside outside of Paris and painted somber landscapes in heavy impasto. In 1906, he returned to Montmartre and began depicting city streets and suburbs in light tones. From 1908 until 1914, when he was frequently in and out of sanitariums, Utrillo worked in what is known as his "white period." By mixing plaster, glue, and cement with his paint, he created whites with which he captured the luminous effects of sunlight on the stucco walls of the city. Painted while he was in treatment in the Sannois sanitarium, this richly textured image is typical of the period. With applications of granular pigment, the artist rendered the gritty, sandy-colored street and the rough off-white plaster surfaces of the architecture. The receding avenue, sidewalks, and flat façades of the buildings lead the viewer's eye into the distance. With its empty streets and leafless trees, *Vue de Sannois* exudes a feeling of loneliness and isolation.

KVG

Auguste Rodin
French, 1840-1917
Portrait of Étienne Clémentel, 1916-1917
Bronze
22 3/4 " x 22 1/4 " x 10 1/2 " (57.8 cm x 56.5 cm x 26.7 cm)
Signed: on the figure's left shoulder
Gift of Mr. Morrie A. Moss 88.1.1

French sculptor and draftsman Auguste Rodin was born in Paris to working-class parents. As a teen he studied at the Petite École (École Spéciale de Dessin et de Mathématiques), where he learned to draw and sculpt in clay. Although a successful student, he failed to gain admission to the École des Beaux-Arts, and was forced to earn his living as a craftsman and embellisher, working for various jewelers, artisans, and masons. Rodin continued to work on his own art, but his early years were a persistent struggle to become a recognized sculptor. On a trip to Italy in 1875, he was inspired by the works of Michelangelo and Donatello, and he felt a new freedom from the stifling academicism of his decorative work.

Following his Italian sojourn, Rodin began to create sculptures that portrayed the human form through an expressive realism. He created many portraits of acquaintances and friends, as well as large public monuments in clay, marble, and bronze. It was through the external appearance that Rodin suggested the character of the sitter. Stressing the materiality of the medium and creating nuances of light and shadow across surfaces, his works became the sculptural equivalent of Impressionist painting.

Through modeling techniques and the rough treatment of surface textures, the *Portrait of Étienne Clémentel* reveals the sitter's strong character in his pensive gaze, forceful jawline, and tight-pursed lips. A successful French statesman, Clémentel (1864-1936) held various cabinet-level positions, including minister of commerce and industry. A psychological study, this work captures the essence of the private man inside the public official. In his furrowed brow and wrinkled eyes, Rodin's characterization depicts the toll of the pressures and demands on the high-ranking government officer. Meeting late in life, the two shared many common interests, including art and poetry, and became close friends. Later Rodin asked Clémentel to sit for a portrait, for which he refused payment. The *Portrait of Étienne Clémentel* was the last sculpture that Rodin completed before his death from a stroke in 1917.

KVG

Chaim Soutine
Russian (School of Paris), 1893-1943
Portrait of Madame Castaing, 1928
Oil on canvas
18 1/2" x 18 1/4" (47 cm x 46.4 cm)
Signed: lower right
Memphis Brooks Museum of Art Purchase 94.8

Born into a large and impoverished Jewish family in Lithuania, Chaim Soutine moved to France at the age of twenty against his father's wishes. He briefly attended the Academy of Fine Arts in Vilno and the École des Beaux-Arts in Paris where he began a close, lifelong friendship with fellow artists Amedeo Modigliani and Marc Chagall. Combining his interests in Expressionism and Fauvism, Soutine's canvases capture the emotion generated by the subject through distorted compositions and intense color. He worked without much recognition until Philadelphia collector Albert Barnes purchased a number of his paintings in 1920. It was Barnes who introduced Soutine to art enthusiasts in America and France, including the wealthy French socialite Madame Castaing. She and her husband, Marcellin, became Soutine's close friends and principal patrons, amassing the finest collection of his paintings. After the artist's death, the Castaings ceased collecting.

Portrait of Madame Castaing conveys the refined elegance of Soutine's patron. Whereas so many of his figures tended to be generalized, this portrait gives evidence of direct observation, particularly through her distinctive face. For all of its specificity the portrait is, nevertheless, characteristic of Soutine's style. The lush application of paint is combined with a modernist emphasis on the dramatic contrast of warm and cool colors, the vibrancy of her flesh registered against the cool blue background. Although his subject avoids eye contact, Soutine's bravura style emphatically draws viewers' attention.

AV & MP

AMERICAN ART
1700-1945

Possibly from the workshop of Benjamin Frothingham
American (Charlestown, Massachusetts), 1734-1809
High Chest of Drawers, ca. 1760-1775
Walnut, pine
83" x 38 3/4" x 20 7/8" (210.8 cm x 98.4 cm x 53 cm)
Bequest of Julie Isenberg 87.20.36

The most commanding piece of furniture in a colonial American home was the high chest of drawers, or highboy as it is popularly known, which was used in a bedroom to store household linens and clothing. It was often accompanied by a matching dressing table, though few have survived together. The high chest was first introduced from England into Boston, the most populous and prosperous city in early-18th-century America. Initially rectilinear with a flat top and six turned legs connected by stretchers, the high chest was dramatically transformed around 1730 by the adoption of the curvilinear Queen Anne, or late Baroque, style which reached its zenith in the conservative Boston area. It remained fashionable there for fifty years, long after the Chippendale, or Rococo, style had supplanted it elsewhere.

This graceful piece was made in the Boston area between 1760 and 1775 in the fully mature Queen Anne style. Parallel movement begins on each side in the simple rounded pad feet and ascends the gently curving cabriole legs along the straight sides to the powerful arched scrolled pediment. The vertical thrust of the chest culminates in the elongated plinth, supporting a corkscrew-shaped finial that arises from the rounded openings in the center of the pediment. The bonnet top created by enclosing the pediment at the rear, the three flattened arches of the skirt separated by turned pendants, and the use of walnut as the primary wood are notable characteristics of Boston-area high chests of this period. Decoration of Queen Anne furniture was subordinated to form. The walnut surfaces of the Brooks' high chest are enhanced largely by the attractive figure of the wood, carved fans on the large central drawers at top and bottom, and the brass hardware.

The back-plate of one of the drawer pulls is stamped "I·GOLD," for John Gold, a brass founder who worked in Birmingham, England, between about 1760 and 1770. Furniture hardware stamped by Gold is found on only two other pieces, one of which is a strikingly similar high chest in the Winterthur Museum that is signed by Benjamin Frothingham, of Charlestown, Massachusetts, whose work is the most fully documented of any Boston-area cabinetmaker of the period. The presence of Gold's hardware on both pieces, along with a close similarity in form and many details, suggests that the Brooks' chest may also have been made in Frothingham's workshop.

WRB

Associated with Daniel Goddard

American (Newport, Rhode Island), 1747-?
Tallcase Clock, ca. 1770-1785
Mahogany
88" x 19" x 10" (223.5 cm x 48.3 cm x 25.4 cm)
Bequest of Julie Isenberg 87.20.34

Prior to the American Revolution, Newport, Rhode Island, was a prosperous seaport whose wealthy merchants created a demand for fine furniture that resulted in the production of some of the most notable pieces in 18th-century America. Two families, the Townsends and the Goddards, dominated furniture making in this city for more than a half century. They often intermarried, and their workshops produced furniture that is uniquely American in design and is superbly crafted. Their original designs and unique sculptural forms rivaled the finest accomplishments of English craftsmen.

The case of this clock exhibits the most distinctive characteristic of the Goddard-Townsend workshops—the blending of raised blocking with an undulating, multilobed shell on the door. While the use of the shell was common to the work of the entire family, the distinctive treatment of this shell is identical to that on a chest signed by Daniel Goddard. The thirteen concave lobes radiating from a central rosette of seven petals allows its attribution to his hand.[1] The reserved yet powerful effect of this piece in the Baroque style is enhanced by the use of finely grained West Indian mahogany, the delicate ogee bracket feet, and the architectural hood with its fluted columns, heavily molded arched pediment, and flame-shaped finials, which provide a final vertical dynamism.

The movement of the clock is unsigned. The painted dial, however, was imported from England and is stamped on the back-plate with the name of James Wilson, one of the earliest recorded makers of painted dials. Wilson worked in Birmingham between 1778 and about 1809.

WRB

[1] Michael Moses, *Master Craftsmen of Newport: The Townsends and Goddards* (Tenafly, New Jersey: MMI Americana Press, 1984), pp. 271-272, 297.

Abraham Dubois
American (Philadelphia), active ca. 1777-1807
Tea Service, ca. 1785-1795
Silver
Teapot: 10 4/8" x 10 5/8" x 5 1/4" (27.6 cm x 27 cm x 13.3 cm)
Cream pitcher: 7 1/4" x 5 3/4" x 3 1/8" (18.4 cm x 14.6 cm x 8 cm)
Sugar basin: 10 1/4" x 4 3/8" x 4 3/8" (26 cm x 11.1 cm x 11.1 cm)
Gift of Mrs. C.M. Gooch 67.16.1-3

This Neoclassical tea service, made in Philadelphia by Abraham Dubois between about 1785 and 1795, was greatly influenced by important social, technological, and stylistic changes in late-18th-century America. Increased formality in social life altered the manner in which tea was consumed. Long a daily activity, serving tea was transformed among the well-to-do elite into an ordered ritual requiring special equipment. Matched tea services such as this one, consisting of three or more pieces, became fashionable and replaced the casually assembled group of individually designed pieces previously used to serve tea.

Technological innovations of the early Industrial Revolution affected the way in which the service was made. Dubois, rather than laboriously flattening and shaping a lump of silver by hand as earlier silversmiths had, was able to purchase long, thin pieces of silver already mechanically flattened by a power-driven rolling mill, recently developed in England. He then cut and bent these to shape, seamed them together, and decorated them with applied strips of mass-produced beading and pierced gallery.

Neoclassicism, embraced in England in the early 1760s, was only adopted in the United States some twenty years later, after the turbulence that reached its climax in the American Revolution. At that time, the ornate, playful Rococo style was supplanted by the restrained, sometimes austere new style that emphasized reason, order, and simplicity—the fundamental principles of the ancient Roman Republic so admired by the Enlightenment and the founders of the new nation. Dubois modeled his teapot and sugar basin on the Roman urn, the defining Neoclassical form, and the cream pitcher on the inverted helmet of a Roman warrior. Also typical of the new style are the square bases; the plain, smooth surfaces decorated only with delicate beading outlining geometrical units; and the engraved symmetrical cartouche containing the owner's initials, "JEK." The architectural pierced gallery of the teapot and sugar basin is a feature found only on Neoclassical silver made in the Philadelphia area.

WRB

Ephraim Mallard
American (Gilmanton, New Hampshire), ca. 1789-1874(?)
Chest of Drawers, ca. 1810-1812
Birch with birch, maple, and mahogany veneers; light and dark wood inlays
37 5/8" x 40 1/2" x 20 3/4" (95.6 cm x 102.9 cm x 52.7 cm)
Signed: interior
Gift of the Decorative Arts Trust 92.4

This piece is a fine example of a group of chests made in the early 19th century in southeastern New Hampshire. Several significant decorative devices are combined to produce one of the most striking façades found in American Neoclassical furniture. Each bowed drawer front is framed by a dark mahogany banding enclosing a symmetrical arrangement of two panels of bird's-eye maple veneer that flank a narrower central panel of highly figured birch, which is separated from the outer panels by a checkered inlay. The central panels, whose feather-like figure forms a vertical line, terminate at the base of the chest in a matching drop panel pendant that also serves as the focal point of the carefully designed apron. Both the pendants and the tall bracket feet with a slight flare at the bottom are distinctive characteristics of Federal period chests made in southeastern New Hampshire.

Unlike most surviving early American furniture, this chest is signed in chalk by its maker, Ephraim Mallard, on five interior surfaces. Mallard may have served his apprenticeship in Portsmouth, the most important urban center north of Boston, and may have worked briefly there after its conclusion. About 1810 or 1811, he moved to Gilmanton, a town north of Portsmouth where he opened a cabinet shop. That this chest was probably made after Mallard's move to this smaller inland community with a less prosperous and sophisticated clientele than Portsmouth is suggested by the contrast of the plain solid birch sides and wide overhanging top with the elaborate veneered façade that would rival in quality of its decoration and craftsmanship any made in the larger city during the Federal period. Mallard had a long career, since he is still recorded as maintaining a workshop in 1849.

The die-stamped brass back-plates of the drawer handles were probably made in Birmingham, England, for the American market. The flying eagle with trailing banner inscribed "E PLURIBUS UNUM" flanked by sixteen stars suggests the back-plates were made between 1796 and 1803, the dates of the admission of the 16th and 17th states to the Union.

WRB

South Jersey Type
American (probably New Jersey or New York)
Pitcher, ca. 1830-1850
Aquamarine non-lead glass
7 7/8" x 7 3/4" x 5 7/8" (20 cm x 19.7 cm x 14.9 cm)
Transferred from Memphis Pink Palace Museum through the
Memphis Glass Collectors Club 56.131

Possibly Boston and Sandwich Glass Company
American (Sandwich, Massachusetts), 1825-1888
Covered Butter Dish, ca. 1830-1840
Colorless lead glass
4" x 5" (10.2 cm x 12.7 cm)
Transferred from Memphis Pink Palace Museum through the
Memphis Glass Collectors Club 67.117a.b

Probably Boston and Sandwich Glass Company
American (Sandwich, Massachusetts), 1825-1888
Decanter with stopper, ca. 1825-1840
Colorless lead glass
10 3/8" x 4 1/2" (26.3 cm x 11.4 cm)
Gift of Jean L. Whitnack 2000.8.1a.b

Although glass was made in early colonial America, its production was inhibited by the large quantity of superior glass imported from Europe. Embargoes during the War of 1812 and the imposition of a tariff in 1824 greatly restricted importation, and as a consequence domestic glasshouses, springing up from New England to the Midwest, became more profitable and innovative. These pieces illustrate three of the most important types of glass produced in early-19th-century America.

The pitcher is a fine example of South Jersey glassware, which is considered uniquely American. Given this name because it was first made in southern New Jersey at the end of the 18th century, the glassware was subsequently imitated in the Northeast and continued to be produced into the 1870s. In making the pitcher, an artisan first blew molten glass to form, and then, before it had cooled, added more glass to the surface of the pitcher, manipulating it into the abstract "lily pad" decoration on the body and the concentric ribbing on the neck. The pale aquamarine color of the pitcher, long used for windowpanes and bottles, was the most characteristic color of South Jersey glassware.

Blown, molded pattern glass was developed as a less expensive imitation of the fine wheel-cut wares made in Ireland and England. The decanter is typical of those made by the Boston and Sandwich Glass Company, which was founded in 1825 and became one of the first successful, enduring American glasshouses. Molten glass was blown by an artisan into the sides of a full-size metal mold composed of several hinged sections whose interior surfaces were cut with the popular sunburst pattern.

The design impressed on the exterior of the finished decanter—once it was released from the mold—was flatter and less sharply delineated than the deeply cut geometric designs on the more expensive imported English and Irish cut glass pieces.

In the late 1820s, a development in America revolutionized the method of making glass for the first time since the introduction of the blowpipe in ancient Rome. A craft in which each piece was individually made by the artisan's breath was transformed into a mechanized industry that rapidly produced large quantities of attractive, inexpensive wares. This rare covered butter dish was made using this process. Molten glass was pressed by machine into the sides of a patterned mold with the background stippled to hide impurities. The "lacy" pressed glass butter dish that emerged was more elaborately decorated than blown molded glass, as well as being less expensive. For the first time glass tableware became available to a wide population.

WRB

Ralph E.W. Earl
American, 1788-1838
Portrait of General Andrew Jackson, President of the United States, 1833
Oil on canvas
36 1/8" x 29 1/8" (91.8 cm x 74 cm)
Signed and dated: lower right
Memphis Park Commission Purchase 46.2

The status of Andrew Jackson as a national icon is well represented in numerous portraits that Ralph E.W. Earl produced over the course of their twenty-year friendship. Earl, son of Connecticut painter Ralph Earl, first visited Jackson at the Hermitage in Nashville in 1817, two years after returning from Europe where he had received training in London under John Trumbull and Benjamin West. While Earl completed his first portrait of the renowned hero of New Orleans, the two men became close friends. The following year, the artist married Jackson's niece and settled in Nashville, becoming one of the first resident portrait painters in Tennessee.

When Jackson was elected to the presidency in 1828, Earl accompanied him to the White House. For the next eight years the artist, dubbing himself the "king's painter," continued to fill the insatiable demand for likenesses of the celebrated leader. The Brooks' portrait, one of the rare canvases that Earl signed and dated, was painted in 1833 for Sir Edward Thomason, an English inventor and merchant. This image reveals Earl's limited ability as a draftsman in regard to perspective and proportion. The modeling of the head—with its strong facial features, billowing white hair, and gallant expression—however, provides a striking impression that Earl replicated on nearly all of his presidential images. The capitol building shown in the distance to the right lends a stately air to the work, while the fading sky at dusk, which fills the background, adds a dimension of drama. The scabbard's inscription, "Our Federal Union—it must be preserved," is taken from a toast Jackson made at a banquet in 1830 commemorating Thomas Jefferson's birthday.

Although Jackson sat for many other prominent American artists, such as John Vanderlyn, Asher B. Durand, and Thomas Sully (who is represented in the Brooks Collection), none could match the output of Earl, who completed more than thirty Jackson portraits in his lifetime. Earl died in 1838, a few years after he left Washington with the former president, and was buried on the grounds of the Hermitage.

MM

Thomas Doughty
American, 1793-1856
Anthony's Nose, Lake George, New York, 1837-1838
Oil on canvas
30 1/8" x 42 1/8" (76.5 cm x 107 cm)
Signed and dated: lower left
Memphis Park Commission Purchase 46.1

Thomas Doughty, one of the pioneers of American landscape painting, exhibited work at the Pennsylvania Academy of the Fine Arts as early as 1816. Born and raised in Philadelphia, he gave up his profession as a leather worker in 1820 to dedicate himself to painting. He studied European landscapes in the collection of his patron, Robert Gilmor Jr. of Baltimore, and then applied this knowledge to the scenery of the eastern United States. Doughty relied upon his innate drawing ability and love of nature to capture the visual and spiritual beauty of rural 19th-century America.

In the fall of 1837 the artist traveled to London, at which time he produced very few canvases of English scenery. Rather, he continued to paint American landscapes that were composed from previous sketches and his own recollections, such as *Anthony's Nose, Lake George*. Upon his return in May of 1838 he took up residence in New York, where, aside from a second trip abroad from 1845 to 1847, he spent the remainder of his life.

Over the course of his career, Doughty moved from a strict imitation of nature to the practice of reordering nature to his own satisfaction. *Anthony's Nose* was painted at mid-career and reflects the artist's somewhat formulated approach to creating his scenes: a body of water with feathery arabesque trees in the foreground, a brilliant light source, and misty hills in the distance. Small figures placed along the shore for scale also suggest man's place in relation to the vast wilderness. Doughty's deep conviction that nature's majesty was a manifestation of God's boundless power and glory was drawn from his friend William Cullen Bryant. This sentiment also epitomizes the attitude of the Hudson River School artists who were to follow.

MM

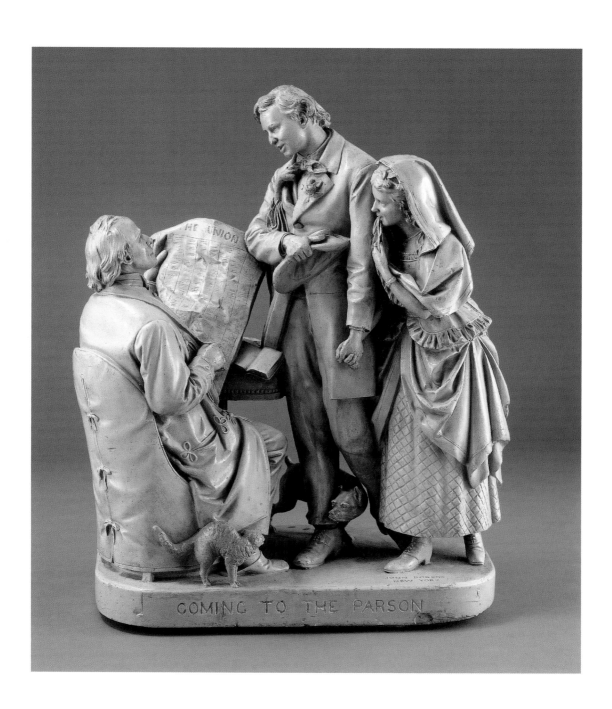

COMING TO THE PARSON

John Rogers
American, 1829-1904
Coming to the Parson, ca. 1870
Plaster
21 3/4" x 16 3/4" x 9 3/4" (55.2 cm x 42.5 cm x 24.7 cm)
Signed and dated: base
Gift of the Brooks Art Gallery League 50.12

When *Coming to the Parson* was released in 1870, it was priced at $15 and eventually sold 8,000 copies. It had all of the hallmarks of John Rogers' most successful sculptures: it depicted a sentimental subject that was easy to understand, was naturalistically rendered, and was affordably priced for a middle-class audience. Between 1860 and 1893, he sold approximately 80,000 plaster copies of groups depicting literary themes, genre scenes, or social commentary.

Born to a leading Boston family, Rogers was well educated although not wealthy. He trained as a mechanic and taught himself to model clay in the evenings. Almost immediately, he attracted attention for his tableaux of ordinary figures. It was not until 1858 that he was able to travel to Europe to study. Unlike such American expatriate sculptors as Randolph Rogers, William Wetmore Store, and Harriet Hosmer, who carved ideal subjects, Rogers was committed to returning to the United States and producing genre scenes.

Rogers' experience as a machinist made the possibilities of mass-producing his sculptures evident. In New York, he mastered the process of making flexible molds and translated *The Slave Auction* (1859) into plaster. Soon, besides selling through galleries and stores, he established a successful mail-order business that reached far beyond the eastern seaboard. The subjects he chose had wide appeal and could not offend even the most prim sensibilities. The poignant scene in *Coming to the Parson* captures a young couple who have surprised a preacher reading his paper, *The Union.* The bride shyly peers out from behind her fiancé, while he addresses the clergyman. Such details as the shawl in her mouth and their tightly clasped hands communicate quickly and evocatively the desire of this bashful couple. Rogers' attention to quotidian elements, including the cat and dog playing around the feet of the men, brings the scene to vivid life.

MP

George Inness
American, 1825-1894
Midsummer, ca. 1874-1876
Oil on canvas
18 1/8" x 26 1/4" (46 cm x 66.5 cm)
Signed: lower right
Gift of Mr. and Mrs. Morrie A. Moss 59.14

During his lifetime, George Inness was considered one of the finest landscape painters in America. With a minimum of training—a month under the tutelage of Regis F. Gignoux and three drawing courses at the National Academy of Design—he began his career as a landscape painter in the 1840s. Initially his work displayed precise brushstrokes with careful attention to detail, drawn from the classical style of Claude Lorrain. After a second trip to Europe in 1853, he adopted the looser brushwork and rural themes of the Barbizon school. Deeply spiritual and intellectual, Inness became an ardent follower of Swedenborgianism in the 1860s. Emanuel Swedenborg's philosophical tenets profoundly influenced Inness, particularly in his later work, as he sought to express nature's inner spiritual life that existed within the realm of physical appearances.

Midsummer is one of numerous scenes Inness painted of Étretat on the Normandy coast—a popular site where he spent the summer of 1874.[1] With sheep grazing in the hills, the cliffs of Étretat appear in the small clearing to the right, with a glimpse of the sea beyond. A solitary figure, a common trait in Inness' work, looks contemplatively into the picture plane. Softly mottled areas of green and ocher, which suggest grass and bushes in the foreground and the distant rolling hills, are divided by tall, sinewy tree trucks. Their dark silhouettes, topped with lush green leaves, are placed at carefully spaced intervals and provide the only linear elements in the painting.

In this work the artist begins to dissolve the edges of shapes, merging them gently, one into another, achieving an ambiguous sense of space. By lessening the distinction between objects and the atmosphere that surrounds them, Inness alludes to the notion of a unifying spiritual force that embodies all things in the material world. In the following years, this softening effect is more pronounced as the artist's visionary landscapes become enveloped in an overall atmospheric haze that obliterates all detail—a style later termed Tonalism.

MM

[1] This scene is identified as Étretat by Michael Quick in his forthcoming *George Inness: A Catalogue Raisonne*; publication date: spring 2005. Quick also suggests that this canvas may have been reworked 1875-1876.

Winslow Homer
American, 1836-1910
Reading by the Brook, 1879
Oil on canvas
15 7/8" x 22 3/4" (40.3 cm x 57.8 cm)
Signed and dated: lower right
Memphis Park Commission Purchase 43.22

From Prouts Neck, Maine, to the tropics of the Caribbean, Winslow Homer recorded a broad range of outdoor scenes with a personal vision and an honest realism. His own observations of men hunting in the Adirondacks, farm girls herding sheep, and fishermen battling the sea served as inspiration for the images he painted directly from nature in watercolors and oils. Homer's early experience as an illustrator in his hometown of Boston accounts for the naturalistic rendering and the storytelling quality in many of his scenes. His intuitive handling of the brush, the fine arrangement of the compositions, and a sympathetic portrayal of the subjects, however, take them beyond mere pictorial narratives.

Homer's only formal training consisted of classes at the National Academy of Design, which he attended periodically from 1859 to 1863. He also made two trips overseas in 1867 and 1881 that exposed him to current trends in European painting. Although Homer never acknowledged any stylistic influences, correlations can be seen in the work of Jules Breton, Eugene Boudin (represented in the Brooks Collection), and Gustave Courbet.

In the late 1870s, Homer produced a series of paintings of young women pursuing various pastimes. Just as in *Reading by the Brook*, many of these figures were portrayed individually, in a quiet, intimate setting. Here, a seated girl, simply rendered, conveys a mood of quiet contemplation. This work demonstrates Homer's masterful ability to take commonplace occurrences and transform them into iconic images. To accomplish this effect, Homer refined his vision to include only those aspects that express the essential character of the scene. In this composition he simplified forms organizing the water, grass, and foliage into three horizontal green bands. Dappled effects of light and shade are reduced to short, flat stokes of color, applied in an Impressionist manner. Dashes of brilliant red and white add a spark of life to the shadowed figure, whose face, hidden from view, adds a further element of timelessness to the scene. This canvas was painted at a midpoint in Homer's career, a time when he was considered by many to be one of the finest genre painters in America.

MM

Ralph Blakelock
American, 1847-1919
Sunset, ca. 1879-1883
Oil on canvas
27 1/4" x 37" (69 cm x 94 cm)
Signed: lower right
Gift of Mr. And Mrs. Morrie A. Moss 58.9

Divine solitude and stillness are embodied in the landscapes of Ralph Blakelock, which were a distillation of his personal experiences in the primeval forests of the United States' western territories. Blakelock first traveled west in 1869 and made a second journey in 1872. Carrying his sketchbook, he lived among Native Americans and became intimately acquainted with their customs and the environment in which they lived. Upon his return, his work slowly progressed from a clear and precise rendering of nature, typical of the Hudson River school, to a more symbolic, less literal depiction. Blakelock's profound reverence for nature found new meaning in the spiritualism of Emanuel Swedenborg, who professed that a divine vital force permeated all living things. In attempting to convey nature's inner life force, Blakelock began utilizing a more painterly and expressive approach to his landscapes. His palette, which became increasingly subdued, was veiled with multiple layers of glazing that created an aura of mysticism.

Sunset, shown at the *Panama-Pacific Exposition* in 1915, was one of many luminous pictures of moonlit vistas, sunsets, and "Indian encampments" that Blakelock produced from 1875 to 1890. In this serene landscape the few narrative elements— a male figure, Native Americans, tepees, and canoes—are barely discernible, as the artist's concern for the painted surface and the mood it evokes begins to take precedence. The dense forest, thickly applied in rich browns and greens, reflects the iridescent glow of the wide-open sky. The fiery orange sun resting on the horizon enhances the mysterious atmosphere of the scene.

Blakelock, a self-taught, independent painter, was categorized by critics as an Impressionist, a Symbolist, a Tonalist, and a romantic visionary. Although difficult to label, his innovative landscapes, drawn from memory and imagination, helped steer the course of American art toward abstraction.

MM

Childe Hassam
American, 1859-1935
Apple Blossoms, ca. 1885
Oil on wood panel
13 3/8" x 15 1/4" (33.8 cm x 38.8 cm)
Signed: lower right
Gift of Walter M. Rentschler 67.1

Childe Hassam, who believed an artist "should paint his own time," chronicled the scenes and events he witnessed through a series of watercolors, oils, and etchings. Born in Massachusetts in 1859, he worked as an illustrator in Boston before touring European art galleries and studios in 1883. His early work from this period reflects the Barbizon school's preference for rural themes, prevalent among the many artists working in Boston. He also painted a series of urban street scenes characterized by hazy atmospheres in the manner of *juste-milieu* (middle-of-the-road) painters Giuseppe de Nittis and Jean Beraud. After a second trip to Paris, where he attended the Académie Julian from 1886 to 1889, Hassam began to employ the rapid, broken brushstrokes and brighter palette of the French Impressionists. When he returned to the United States, this became his signature style and, along with Theodore Robinson, John Henry Twachtman, and J. Alden Weir, he was one of the leading proponents of Impressionism in America.

In depicting the seaports and villages of New England, or the cityscapes of New York, Boston, or Chicago, Hassam's work reflects his interest in light and the effects of weather. This small panel of an apple orchard, painted early in his career, captures a fleeting seasonal moment as blossoms flutter in the breeze and a few petals gently tumble to the ground. In some respects it appears Impressionistic—the quick, short brushstrokes of the flowers, in soft pink with touches of salmon and daubs of green leaves, give the effect of reflected light and movement. Yet Hassam still employs broader, sweeping strokes in muted shades of green for the field and the trees on the distant horizon, aspects still retained from his exposure to the French Barbizon school. The immediacy of Hassam's painting technique gives it the appearance of a quick study, yet the work is carefully composed. Tree by tree, the composition leads us back into the picture plane to the white house at the center of the horizon.

MM

Carl Gutherz
American (b. Switzerland), 1844-1907
Light of the Incarnation, 1888
Oil on canvas
77" x 114" (195.6 cm x 289.6 cm)
Signed and dated: lower right
Gift of Mr. and Mrs. Marshall F. Goodheart 68.11.1

Carl Gutherz, a Swiss-born American artist, was among the small group of Tennessee artists who took up residence in Paris in the last quarter of the 19th century. Leaving Memphis in 1870, he received his initial training at the École des Beaux-Arts in Paris. Upon his return to the United States, he became an art instructor in St. Louis from 1875 to 1884, helping to establish the St. Louis School and Museum of Fine Arts (today the St. Louis Art Museum). During his second tenure in Paris, from 1884 to 1896, he attended the Académie Julian under French masters Jules Lefebvre and Gustave Boulanger. His work took on a new direction and inspiration as he combined his Christian beliefs with Symbolist imagery and ideology, producing some of his finest large-scale salon paintings. Returning to the United States in 1896 to work on a set of murals for the Library of Congress, Gutherz and his family settled in Washington, D.C., where he remained until his death in 1907.

Light of the Incarnation, which received a bronze medal in the1889 Paris *Exposition Universelle*, was Gutherz's most successful and widely exhibited painting. It is one of a number of canvases where he explored the link between the spiritual world and earthly existence, between the real and the ideal. It reflects the 19th-century Symbolist aesthetic that put an emphasis upon imagination, intuition, and the senses, and also explored the realms of divinity and the supernatural.

Here, the birth of Christ is seen from the perspective of the angels above, as the "heavenly Host unites in rejoicing" and "light glows back from earth to heaven."[1] From the lofty clouds, an angel with outstretched arms beckons us to witness this miraculous event. Gutherz chose opalescent colors to paint this immense ethereal scene, using flowers, birds, and butterflies as symbols of purity and rebirth. The elegantly posed and draped figures owe much to his admiration for Raphael, while the halos in gilt relief, which lend a decorative element to the surface, recall the work of Renaissance artists such as Fra Angelico.

MM

[1]Carl Gutherz, *Green Journal* (unpublished notebook), Collection of Memphis Brooks Museum of Art, p. 122.

Edward A. Bell
American, 1862-1953
Lady in Gray, 1889
Oil on canvas
76 1/8" x 49 1/2" (193.4 cm x 125.7 cm)
Signed: lower left
Gift of the artist 33.1

Lady in Gray, Edward A. Bell's most celebrated work, was painted during his ten-year residency in Munich. A native New Yorker, Bell went abroad in 1881 and studied at the Bavarian Royal Academy. He was trained in the Munich style of painting that favored realistic portraiture and historical scenes rendered with thick brushstrokes in warm brown tones, derived from Baroque masters such as Diego Velázquez and Frans Hals. Bell's early work from this period reflects this influence, as well as that of William Merritt Chase (see page 172), also a Munich graduate, who was Bell's instructor at New York's Art Students League from 1879 to 1881.

The majority of Bell's work is figurative; many of his later paintings depict graceful female subjects. These women, elegantly dressed and set in decorative interiors that often include objets d'art, are similar to the romantic style and subject matter of Belgian painter Alfred Stevens, who also inspired Chase. In contrast, *Lady in Gray*, with its simple draped background, fur rug, life-size format, and narrow tonal range, correlates more closely with James McNeill Whistler's *Symphony in White, No. 1: The White Girl* (1862).[1] Bell's young model, gazing wide-eyed at the viewer, is portrayed unpretentiously in a plain gray blue dress before a gray background of nearly the same value. The plush white rug rendered in thick feathery strokes accentuates the dark hemline of the dress, while the flesh tones, ocher hat, and pink ribbon and flowers provide subtle contrast. The painting's cooler and lighter palette was a departure from that of the Munich school, but the artist's broad, textured brushstrokes and realistic interpretation of the subject still reflect his Munich training. The title, which includes the predominant color scheme of the work, is also a Whistlerian trait.

This portrait depicts a seventeen-year-old music conservatory student who went on to become a successful concert singer, but was later killed during the post-World War I riots in Munich. The painting received silver medals at both the *Bavarian Royal Academy Exposition* and the Paris *Exposition Universelle* in 1889. It was also included in the 1893 Chicago *World's Columbian Exposition* and the *Tennessee Centennial and International Exposition* in Nashville in 1897.

MM

[1]Lacey Taylor Jordan in Linda Merrill, *After Whistler: The Artist and His Influence on American Painting* (Atlanta, Georgia: High Museum of Art, 2003), pp. 142-143.

Tiffany & Co.
American (New York)
Pair of Ewers, 1891-1902
Silver
21 5/8" X 10 5/8" X 7 1/4" (54.9 cm x 27 cm x 18.4 cm)
Gift of the Decorative Arts Trust 2001.2.1-2

American silver design and craftsmanship reached its zenith at the end of the 19th century in the workshops of Tiffany & Co. Originally established as a fancy goods retailer in New York City in 1837, the firm began to manufacture silver in 1851, and eventually became the largest producer of silver in America, selling pieces both here and abroad.

These imposing ewers were made between 1891 and 1902, in what the Tiffany plant journal called a Roman design, which was introduced about 1882. Their form and decoration are based on a 16th-century northern European Mannerist interpretation of classical antiquity. The decoration is a bacchanalian scene associated with wine. Panels chased in high relief around the body of the ewers show *putti* engaging in various types of revelry: playing instruments, dancing, and drinking from a goblet. A separately cast reclining *putto* holding a bunch of grapes to his lips is fixed at the apex of each handle, and trailing grapevines are applied to the base and body of the pieces.

While used for serving wine in a ceremonial manner at a grand function, ewers of this monumental size (nearly twenty-two inches in height with a capacity of nine pints) and elaborate decoration were displayed on a sideboard or used to pour at table. They provided dramatic visual evidence of the wealth, social standing, and aesthetic sophistication of the owner. Their status as a luxury item is borne out by a plant ledger entry of 1895, which indicates that a single "pitcher Roman large" weighing 96.5 troy ounces of sterling silver cost $400 to produce.[1]

WRB

[1] *Silver Manufacturing Ledger* entry 7082 of September 5, 1895, Tiffany & Co. Archives, Parsippany, New Jersey.

Archibald M. Willard
American, 1836-1918
Minute Men, ca. 1895
Oil on linen
36" x 50.4" (91.4 cm x 128 cm)
Signed: lower right
Gift of the Paul and Elissa Cahn Foundation 2003.12

Archibald M. Willard was born in Ohio, where he worked as a carriage and furniture painter. In 1863 he enlisted in the 86th Ohio Volunteer Infantry. During the Civil War, he illustrated battle scenes and befriended the photographer and entrepreneur James F. Ryder, who encouraged Willard to sell photographic copies of his drawings. The royalties from the sales afforded Willard sufficient income to travel to New York City and study art. His talents were quickly recognized and within a year he exhibited at the National Academy of Design. Willard's career blossomed after his well-known painting *The Spirit of '76* was displayed at the 1876 Philadelphia *Centennial* Exhibition. Originally titled *Yankee Doodle*, the painting portrays a drum and fife corps that was responsible for relaying instructions to soldiers, directing the troop's movement, and providing inspiration to the military forces during the war.

Continuing to work within the genre of history painting, Willard depicts a soldier's painful but patriotic duty in *Minute Men*. The image is a narrative that illustrates and memorializes the heroic spirit of the men who fought in the Revolutionary War. A man, interrupted while chopping wood, and his wife gaze out across the expansive countryside toward a skirmish developing on the bridge below. The family gathers around him in anticipation of his departure for battle. The dramatic connection created between the family and the wide-open panorama in the background symbolizes the importance of the land to the burgeoning nation. A simple scene of leave-taking, *Minute Men* both links and celebrates family, home, and country.

AV

Edward S. Curtis
American, 1868-1952
***Getting Water—Apache* from *The North American Indian*,** 1903
Photogravure
15 1/4 " x 11 7/8 " (38.7 cm x 30.2 cm)
Gift of Mr. and Mrs. O.M. Bennett 41.17

Frontier photographer Edward S. Curtis grew up in Minnesota and Washington State. He developed an interest in photography in his teens, and commenced a successful career as a portraitist in Seattle before beginning his twenty-volume photographic series, *The North American Indian* (1907-1930). Endorsed by J.P Morgan and President Theodore Roosevelt, the project was an ambitious attempt to document disappearing Native American traditions. For thirty years, he photographed tribes in the United States, British Columbia, and Alaska.

Though criticized in recent years for their romantic, and sometimes inaccurate, portrayal of Native American life, the images were very popular in the early 20th century. Curtis befriended many of his subjects, who agreed to pose for his often staged tableaux. A master of composition, Curtis draws attention here to the crouching woman through the raking diagonal of the water's edge, contrasted dramatically with the diagonal of her arm. Additionally, the two trees above form a triangle pointing down at her. Through such formal means, Curtis directs viewers' attention to specific artifacts identified with Native American life: the water jug, the horses loaded with baskets, and the blanket the woman is wearing. Perhaps more artful than accurate, *Getting Water—Apache* reveals Curtis' paradoxical ambition to be both artist and anthropologist.

AV & MP

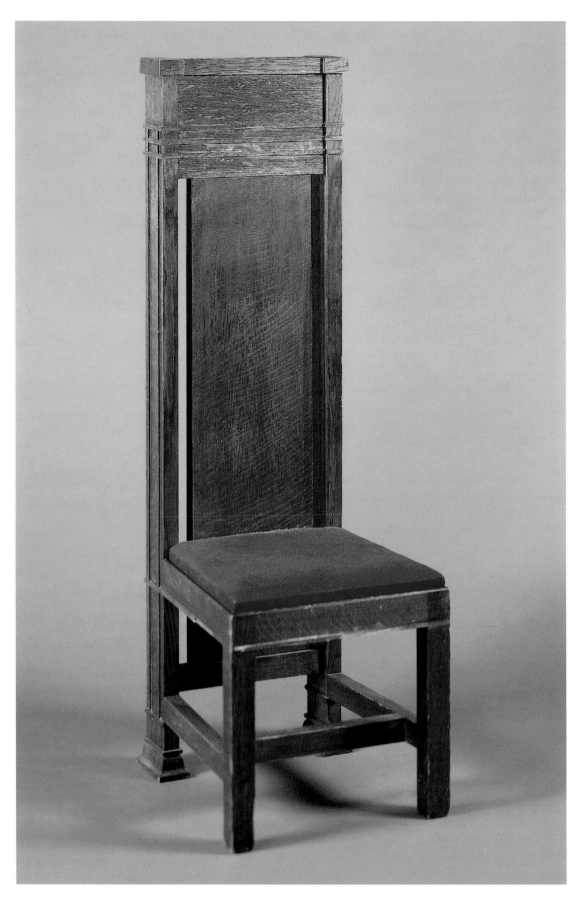

Frank Lloyd Wright
American, 1867-1959
Chair, 1903-1904
Oak
52" x 16 1/4" x 19 1/4" (132.1 cm x 41.3 cm x 48.9 cm)
Memphis Brooks Museum of Art purchase with funds provided through
exchange by Mary Ann Robinson and the Decorative Arts Trust 86.21

Frank Lloyd Wright was perhaps the best-known figure in the emergence in the
20th century of the first distinctly American architecture and design. After working
in the office of the architect Louis Sullivan, Wright opened his own studio in
Chicago in 1893, and soon developed his Prairie School style. He designed low,
horizontally oriented houses with open, uncluttered interior spaces to mirror the
flat midwestern countryside, and created complementary interior fittings and
furniture for many of them that reinforced the feeling of openness and simplicity.

This high-back chair was designed by Wright for the dining room of the Prairie
School style house built in Peoria, Illinois, for Francis W. Little in 1903. Its strong
vertical orientation was intended to balance the horizontal lines of the room, as
well as the table at which it stood. The chair is a powerful combination of rectilinear
elements, making no concessions to the contours of the human body. The solid
back panel between two substantial posts begins at the back stretcher near the
floor, rises above the seat, and terminates in a horizontal panel forming a crest
capped with a simulated cornice. Moldings at the base of the back posts heighten
the architectural effect of the chair. Flat surfaces are broken and softened by narrow
intersecting strips of wood applied to the crest, posts, and base of the seat rail and
by the stretchers. Wright's characteristic commitment to simplicity is evident in the
form of the piece and the plain, solid fabric covering its seat.

The construction of the chair reflects Wright's preference for the use of natural
materials and modern technological innovations. Indigenous white oak was cut
and planed to an even, uniform surface by machine, revealing the wood's
distinctive rays. New industrial technology also made possible the use of more
precisely cut, hidden joints than those found in handcrafted work. The materials,
construction methods, and dark-stained finish matched those used on the walls of
the dining room. Though carefully designed and fabricated to integrate into the
architectural context of the Little House, this chair, when viewed alone, is a striking
piece of sculpture.

WRB

Nonconnah Pottery
American (Shelby County, Tennessee)
Teapot, 1904-1910
Earthenware
5 1/4" x 9 1/2" x 6 3/4" (13.3 cm x 23.2 cm x 17.1 cm)
Gift of the Decorative Arts Trust 2003.4.2a-b

Around 1896, Walter B. Stephen (1875-1961) moved with his parents from Nebraska to a farm south of Memphis in Shelby County, Tennessee, where he worked as a mason and stonecutter. His mother, Nellie (1857-1910), was a successful artist who had drawn illustrations for *The Youth's Companion* and exhibited paintings at the *Tennessee Centennial Exposition* in 1897.

A neighbor who visited the *Louisiana Purchase Exposition* in St. Louis in 1904 told the Stephen family about seeing fascinating demonstrations by a craftsman, probably George Ohr, throwing pots using a wheel. Inspired by these accounts, Walter and his mother began to experiment with interesting multicolored clays recently discovered near their farm. Walter Stephen made pieces using both molds and a wheel, and his mother decorated them with slip-painted botanical designs, animals, birds, and nostalgic scenes of covered wagons and Native Americans. They soon developed a modest commercial operation, selling their pottery largely to friends and neighbors. The Stephens adopted the Native American name of the nearby Nonconnah Creek for their ceramic enterprise.

Practically unrecognized until recently, the small body of surviving examples of Nonconnah Pottery made between 1904 and 1910 is typical of the distinctive work of the Arts and Crafts movement in early-20th-century America. Molded by Walter Stephen, this attractive teapot (one of three pieces in the Brooks Collection) was decorated by Nellie Stephen with a light blue matt ground typical of her work. White frost daisies with green leaves on brown stems are slip-painted on this ground in various levels of relief. This naturalistic floral decoration circles the entire body of the teapot and extends onto the top and handle, unifying its different structural elements.

After his parents' deaths in 1910, Walter Stephen settled in western North Carolina, where he established and operated the well-known Pisgah Forest Pottery until his death in 1961.

WRB

Gorham and Company
American (Providence, Rhode Island)
Pitcher, 1905
Silver (.9584 fine)
8 7/8" x 8 5/8" x 5 5/8" (22.6 cm x 22 cm x 14.3 cm)
Gift of Mrs. Ben Baer 2004.5.2

Gorham and Company, founded in Providence, Rhode Island, in 1831, became, with Tiffany & Co., the leading producer of silverware in 19th-century America. Although relying heavily on industrial production techniques from the beginning, the company departed from this tradition in 1897 by introducing a new line aimed at a rarified market. Influenced by the Arts and Crafts movement, this line was known as Martelé ("hammered" in French), for each piece was individually raised and decorated by hand from silver, which was purer and more malleable than the sterling standard. While the line was developed and overseen by the Englishman William C. Codman, who became Gorham's chief designer in 1891, all objects were specially designed, with the result that none of the approximately 4,800 pieces produced were identical.[1]

This water pitcher, made in 1905 when the production of Martelé reached its height, exemplifies the influence of the fanciful French Art Nouveau style. The emphasis on undulating, organic forms is evident in every aspect of the pitcher's design: the swelling lobe-shaped sides outlined by curved vertical molding, the graceful scalloped everted lip and spout, the double curve of the handle, and the shaped flowing base with lightly rounded lobed feet. The decoration, chased in bold relief and employing motifs drawn from nature, is typical of Art Nouveau. Twining around the body of the pitcher is the climbing plant known as hop (*Humulus lupulus*); its distinctive leaves and the drooping cone-like flowers of the female of the species also decorate the spout and handle, providing added unity to this organic piece.

Because only the wealthy could afford this individually designed and handcrafted silver, the line was discontinued in 1912, although a few special commissions were executed later. During its brief life Martelé exemplified the height of creativity, craftsmanship, and sophistication in American decorative arts, and gained wide recognition by winning prizes in international expositions in Paris, Milan, and St. Louis.

WRB

[1]Harold Newman, *An Illustrated Dictionary of Silverware* (London: Thames & Hudson, 1987), p. 205.

Robert Henri
American, 1865-1929
Cori with Cat, 1907
Oil on canvas
24" x 20" (61 cm x 50.8 cm)
Signed: lower right
Memphis Park Commission Purchase 54.1

Robert Henri was born in Cincinnati, studied at the Pennsylvania Academy of the Fine Arts, and made three trips to Europe between 1888 and 1900, where he studied French art. Working initially in an Impressionist style, he turned to a painterly realism that was informed by the work of Frans Hals, Édouard Manet, and Rembrandt van Rijn (see page 78). The change was not merely superficial. Henri, who exerted an enormous influence as a teacher and as the author of *The Art Spirit* (1923), encouraged American artists to paint in a straightforward style that communicated their enthusiasm for contemporary urban life. Henri and his compatriots, who were known as the Ashcan school, opposed what they saw as the decorative and superficial nature of the Tonalist and American Impressionist artists. Instead, they painted sympathetic images of the city and its dwellers, developing a democratic art with roots in the theories of Walt Whitman and Henry David Thoreau. Beauty could be found in ostensibly vulgar subjects because it was present in life and was therefore a legitimate subject for artists.

Cori with Cat is a fine example of the vibrancy that Henri generated in his paintings through a loose, gestural brushstroke. He encouraged artists to paint quickly as a means of capturing the living presence of the subject, which can be seen in this portrait. The slashing strokes of Cori's shirt and face energize the image and convey the impishness of the sitter, while the simplified blue green background sets off the pinks of her face and shirt, drawing attention to her happy smile. Cori, a Dutch girl who posed for a series of paintings and drawings during the summer of 1907, seems about to run off and play.

MP

Florine Stettheimer
American, 1871-1944
Still Life Number One with Flowers (Flowers Against Wallpaper), ca. 1915
Oil on canvas
36" x 26 1/2" (91.4 cm x 66.4 cm)
Signed: lower left
Gift of the estate of Miss Ettie Stettheimer 60.21

In 1914, the Stettheimer sisters—Carrie, Florine, and Ettie—and their mother, Rosetta Walter, established their salon in New York City after living as American expatriates in Europe for many years. Their soirees were frequented by such artists, intellectuals, and writers as Marsden Hartley, Charles Demuth, Virgil Thomson, Carl Van Vechten, Sherwood Anderson, and Alfred Stieglitz. Adorned with Florine's artworks, their apartments provided a marvelous backdrop for their influential visitors, many of whom ended up as Florine's subjects. Among her idiosyncratic paintings are portraits of Marcel Duchamp and art critic Henry McBride, images of family parties and picnics, and the fantastical series *Cathedrals of: Broadway, Fifth Avenue, Wall Street, and Art* (1929-1944).

Still Life Number One with Flowers is an early work, completed soon after her return from Europe, and before she established her signature style. Stettheimer studied European Modernism in Berlin, Munich, and Paris, and then developed her personal style, one that appeared naïve, and utilized pattern and color to produce abstract and decorative canvases. Here, the thickly painted wallpaper serves as a backdrop for the vases, which declare their three-dimensionality through the shadows they cast. The riot of bird and floral patterns, however, is difficult to disentangle as the flowers in the vases slip into the wallpaper in a typical Modernist play with illusions of space. The stems, leaves, and buds snake through the canvas, creating a skein of color across the surface that seems to throb with life.

Stettheimer and her work were not known widely during her lifetime. After her 1916 exhibition at M. Knoedler & Company received mixed reviews, she refused all invitations, including that of Stieglitz, for another solo display, although she participated in many group shows. She was greatly admired, however, by some of America's most important artists and intellectuals. Upon her death, Duchamp organized a retrospective of her work at the Museum of Modern Art, New York, in 1946 that included *Still Life Number One with Flowers.*

MP

William Merritt Chase
American, 1849-1916
Self-Portrait, 1916
Oil on canvas
20 1/4" x 16 1/2" (51.4 cm x 41 cm)
Gift of the Memphis Art Association 22.1

William Merritt Chase studied in Europe from 1872 to 1877, traveling first to Munich, which was the German art center of the time. There, he studied the painting of Spanish and Dutch masters, including Diego Velázquez and Frans Hals, and developed his characteristic painterly brushwork and dark palette. On his return to the United States, Chase embarked upon a successful career as both artist and teacher. He taught at several schools in New York City and Philadelphia, as well as summers at Shinnecock, Long Island, influencing a generation of artists who went on to work in different styles. Chase became one of the nation's most prominent portraitists, although he was also well known for his landscapes and genre scenes. A facile painter, he ranged stylistically from dark, Baroque-inspired interiors to light-filled, colorful, impressionistic landscapes.

In his late bust-length *Self-Portrait,* Chase presents himself as an elegant gentleman. Everything suggests wealth and ease, from his glasses to the flower in his buttonhole and his grand mustache. Even his position within the canvas connotes power—depicted close to the picture plane, he fills and thoroughly dominates the space. The bravado brushwork that Chase is noted for is evident throughout the portrait, particularly in the cravat and beard. There is nothing, however, to suggest that Chase's wealth comes from his work as a painter.

When the Brooks Memorial Art Gallery opened in 1916, Chase served on the Museum's Acquisitions Committee, along with the artists Cecilia Beaux and Kate Carl (both of whom are represented in the Brooks Collection). This self-portrait was included in a posthumous retrospective at the Metropolitan Museum of Art in 1917, and was acquired by the Brooks in 1922.

MP

Newcomb Pottery (bottom)
American (New Orleans, Louisiana)
Vase, 1927
Earthenware
6 5/8" x 4 7/8" (16.8 cm x 12.4 cm)
Fully marked: base
Bequest of Martha Turley Jack 2003.5.1

Newcomb Pottery (top)
American (New Orleans, Louisiana)
Vase, 1918
Earthenware
13 1/2 " x 5 3/4" (34.3 cm x 14.6 cm)
Fully marked: base
Gift of the Memphis Art League 22.18

The Newcomb Pottery was founded in 1895 at Sophie Newcomb College, the women's unit of Tulane University in New Orleans, as a laboratory where female students could receive practical training to earn a living. A professional male potter was employed to throw the pieces, which were then decorated by student artists. Eventually, the students were joined by a small group of alumnae known as "Art Craftsmen" who worked as professional decorators.

These two vases were thrown by Joseph Meyer, as were virtually all of the pieces produced at the pottery between 1896 and 1927. The taller was decorated by Anna Francis Simpson and the shorter by Sadie Irvine. Both studied at Newcomb from 1902 until 1908, and then became Art Craftsmen. Simpson worked until her death in 1930, and Irvine, who also taught for many years and has been called the greatest of the Newcomb decorators, remained at the pottery until her retirement in 1952.

From the beginning, the Newcomb Pottery insisted that the decoration of each piece be individually designed, and that decorators employ natural motifs that evoked the South and the southern landscape. Initially these were highly stylized incised floral designs with glossy glazes. Shortly before 1910, however, the emphasis shifted to a more realistic treatment. The decoration of these vases, lightly carved in low relief, depicts two variations of the most famous motif of this period originally created by Irvine: a full moon shining through native trees in a landscape. One is decorated with moss-draped willows found in the Louisiana bayou country, and the other with more exotic palms native to south Florida. The dominant use of blue and blue green underpainting beneath a matt glaze was typical of Newcomb work done after the introduction of this glaze at the pottery in 1911, and creates a hazy romantic atmosphere evocative of the Old South.

The Newcomb Pottery was highly successful as an artistic, educational, and commercial endeavor. Its pieces were shown at many international expositions and were marketed widely. The vase by Irvine retains it original sales label on the base indicating a price of $10, a substantial sum at the time.

WRB

George Luks
American, 1867-1933
The Fortune Teller, ca. 1920
Oil on canvas
43 5/8" x 38 7/8 " (110.8 cm x 98.7 cm)
Signed: lower right
Memphis Park Commission Purchase 54.2

George Luks was born in Williamsport, Pennsylvania, and briefly attended the Pennsylvania Academy of the Fine Arts before traveling extensively through Europe in the early 1890s. When he returned to the United States, he joined the *Philadelphia Press* as an illustrator and met other newspaper artists, including Everett Shinn (represented in the Brooks Collection) and Robert Henri (see page 168). It was Luks' experience in journalism that taught him how to render his subjects quickly and accurately. As a member of the Ashcan school, a group of artists who rendered the everyday experiences of urban life, first in Philadelphia and later in New York City, Luks concentrated on the more humble aspects of the city around him, primarily painting the poor and working class.

A familiar figure in Luks' body of work was the fortune-teller. This portrait depicts an elderly woman against a simple background; the subdued colors, which evoke urban grime, probably derive from Dutch and Spanish Baroque precedents. Also like Baroque masters, Luks treated his humble subject with sympathy and respect, as indicated by the large size of the canvas. Through dramatic color contrast, Luks creates two focal points: her coarse, weathered face, and her hand, accordion, handkerchief, and birds. When realized in his characteristic painterly style, the result is a vibrant image of an urban character.

AV & MP

Isaac Soyer
American (b. Russia), 1902-1981
Cafeteria, 1930
Oil on canvas
21 3/8 " x 25 7/8" (54.3 cm x 65.7 cm)
Signed: lower left
Gift of Mr. E.R. Brumley 45.12

Born in Russia, Isaac Soyer immigrated along with his artist brothers Raphael (see page 198) and Moses (represented in the Brooks Collection) to the United States shortly before World War I. During high school, he took evening classes at Cooper Union, and after graduating, studied at the National Academy of Design. He traveled to Europe in 1928, where he was drawn to the old masters at the Louvre. A Social Realist like his brothers, Soyer depicted the urban social and economic difficulties of the Great Depression. As Social Realist art was meant to effect social change, the painting had to be easy to read—abstraction might have obscured the artist's intention. In contrast with the celebration of American life often seen in much of the work of the Regionalists, Soyer sympathetically painted tired shopgirls, absorbed office workers, and scenes of their drab lives.

Along with the lettering "Cafeteria," the phrase "Ladies Invited" appears on the window, a perhaps ironic welcome to the women of the segregated working world. The woman engrossed in reapplying her lipstick after finishing her meal is most likely a secretary on her lunch hour. She is seated next to a man who is probably a white-collar office manager. Oblivious to her presence, he is immersed in his newspaper, which creates a physical barrier between them. Soyer's painting is informed by the work of Edgar Degas, which can be seen here both in the manner that the figures are cut off by the edge of the canvas, and in the emptiness and distance that separates these self-absorbed individuals. The hierarchy of the workplace, where men held positions as managers, supervisors, and executives while women worked as secretaries, clerks, and receptionists with little chance of advancement, is carried over into this scene; larger and occupying more of the picture plane, the man visually dominates the woman. Even the newspaper he is reading invades her area of the canvas, forcing her into the corner. Although the sphere Soyer depicts is not entirely a warm and friendly place, his sympathy for the inhabitants is clear nonetheless.

MP

Thomas Hart Benton
American, 1889-1975
Engineer's Dream, 1931
Oil on canvas
29 7/8" x 41 3/4" (75.9 cm x 106 cm)
Signed: lower left
Eugenia Buxton Whitnel Funds 75.1

In his 1937 autobiography, *An Artist in America*, Thomas Hart Benton wrote, "My first pictures were of railroad trains. Engines were the most impressive things that came into my childhood. To go down to the depot and see them come in, belching black smoke, with their big headlights shining and their bells ringing and their pistons clanking, gave me a feeling of stupendous drama, which I have not lost to this day."

Benton's fascination with trains is evident in *Engineer's Dream*, inspired by a song of the same name written by Carson Robison, America's first cowboy radio singer. A harmonica player, Benton was interested in American folk and country music, and made paintings based on song lyrics. The tune recounts a mythic train wreck through the dream, which turns into a premonition of disaster, of an old man sleeping by a fire. The man's son is a train engineer racing through a stormy night to arrive on time when his train comes to a bridge that has washed out. The closing refrain mournfully states, "And then through the night came a message, and it told him his dream had been true. His brave son had gone to his maker along with the rest of the crew."[1] The canvas is divided diagonally into two sections. In the lower right, the engineer's father dreams of the upcoming disaster. Above him, the monstrous train, incarnating Benton's previously quoted description, roars off the tracks. Unsuccessfully attempting to prevent the calamity, a man waves a warning flag while a figure jumps from the train. The cruciform shape of the telephone pole adds to the drama of the event.

The son of a famous congressman from Missouri, Benton studied at the Art Institute of Chicago before traveling in 1908 to Paris, where he stayed for five years. Upon his return, his paintings were based on European Modernism. Soon, he developed a new American art that addressed local themes painted in a naturalistic style known as Regionalism. Benton was also indebted to the Mannerist art of Michelangelo, El Greco, and Tintoretto. Their example can be seen in the contorted, monumental figure of the engineer; the manner in which objects are abstracted into swirling, curvilinear forms such as the water above the engineer's right knee; and Benton's use of color and value.

MP

[1] Carson J. Robison, *The Engineer's Dream,* (Old Homestead Publishers, 1927).

Arthur Dove
American, 1880-1946
Car in Garage, 1934
Oil on canvas
12 1/4" x 14 1/2" (31.1 cm x 35.9 cm)
Signed: bottom center
Eugenia Buxton Whitnel Funds 76.12

Arthur Dove was born in Canandaigua, New York, and settled in New York City in 1903. There, he worked as a freelance illustrator for magazines such as *Scribner's* and *Harper's.* Following two years in Europe where he encountered European Modernism, Dove returned to New York in 1909. Alfred Stieglitz gave him his first one-person exhibition at Gallery 291 in 1912. Deeply interested in nature and organic forces, Dove produced some of the first distinctly nonobjective, or fully abstract, works by an American artist. He liberated line from illustration to evoke the energy within all living things instead of capturing their exterior appearance.

In *Car in Garage*, the rectangular or square building the viewer might expect to see housing a car is transformed into a curved shape crowned with waves suggesting energy and movement. Represented by an ovoid mass topped by an egg form and a red radiator grill, the car ends with a red bumper below. Objects within the painting grow into each other, making it virtually impossible to distinguish individual elements. Such ambiguity, however, is outweighed by the harmonious and lively composition emphasizing the dynamism of the automobile and the space containing it. The limited palette of earth tones is highlighted with a few powerful areas of color—the white-and-yellow egg, and the red of the grill and bumper. The end result is an animated scene that engages the viewer in a game of deciphering the components Dove cleverly arranged on the canvas. Indeed, were it not for the title, the subject would most likely remain a mystery.

MP

John Steuart Curry
American, 1897-1946
The Hen and the Hawk, 1934
Oil on canvas
26 1/4" x 20 1/4" (66.5 x 51.5 cm)
Signed and dated: upper left
Bequest of Mrs. C.M. Gooch 80.3.17

Born on a farm outside of Dunavant, Kansas, John Steuart Curry was one of the most important American Regionalist painters, along with Grant Wood and Thomas Hart Benton (see page 180). Curry studied art at the Kansas City Art Institute and the Art Institute of Chicago before starting his career as an apprentice magazine illustrator in New Jersey. Subsequently, he spent a year studying in Paris, where he took great interest in the depictions of violent animal fights by Peter Paul Rubens, Eugène Delacroix, and Théodore Géricault. Eventually settling in New York City, Curry began painting scenes from the American heartland. Life in rural America was an important subject for his work, as he believed that art should come from one's daily experiences. Though he never lived in the Midwest again, the familiar images of his childhood on the farm were an important source of inspiration. It was there that Curry developed an affinity for natural phenomena and an admiration for farm animals.

Conflict and the struggle for survival, for humans and animals alike, are significant themes in Curry's work. In *The Hen and the Hawk*, the artist has chosen to depict the most dramatic moment of the narrative, just before the attempted kill. The downward motion of the hawk's attack on the chicks is emphasized by the V-shape created by its outspread wings, and the green zigzag outlines of the trees in the background. Curry draws the viewer's attention to the turmoil in the center of the composition with the brilliant red of the hen's comb and wattles, juxtaposed against her earthy white feathers rendered in convincing textural detail. The hen closes her eyes, leaps off the ground while aiming her talons at the hawk, and fiercely defends her young. The chicks scramble to get away from the ensuing conflict, and as a result, one chick tumbles head over foot in the escape. Curry's portrayal of the hen's fierce protection of her chicks is also a compassionate metaphor for the power of maternal love.

KHD

Anna Hyatt Huntington
American, 1876-1973
Greyhounds Playing, 1936
Bronze
38" x 41 1/4" x 15 1/2" (96.5 cm x 104.8 cm x 39.4 cm)
Signed and dated: lower left
Gift of the artist 38.8

Born in Cambridge, Massachusetts, Anna Hyatt Huntington was the daughter of a prominent zoologist. She developed a lifelong interest in animals, becoming an expert in animal anatomy and behavior. At the age of nineteen, when she turned to sculpture, she chose animals as her subject matter. She studied briefly with Henry K. Kitson in Boston and at the Art Students League in New York, yet her training was mostly self-directed as she learned to sculpt by modeling from live subjects. Huntington's artistic vision did not reflect that of 20th-century Modernism, which often favored abstraction over representation, and the expression of ideas, fantasies, and dreams rather than the depiction of the everyday world. Preferring an academic and realistic approach to subjects, Huntington emphasized the faithful rendering of her models and excellent craftsmanship in her work. She became one of America's greatest sculptors of animals and her output was enormous.

Huntington was the recipient of many honors and awards during her career, including, in 1937, the Widener Gold Medal at the Pennsylvania Academy for *Greyhounds Playing.* In this lifelike portrayal, the artist demonstrates her mastery of animal form, behavior, and nature. The dogs are vibrantly alive as they face one another, gracefully twisting and turning on their hind legs with their backs arched and their muscles taut. The curving, elegant lines of their poses are reminiscent of the flowing lines of the Art Nouveau style. Huntington achieves unity in each angle of the composition—created to be viewed from all sides—through the interplay of positive and negative space. Fusing naturalistic skill with instinctive sympathy for the dogs, she captures not only an anatomically detailed portrait, but also the dogs' inherent grace, beauty, and playfulness.

KVG

Burton Callicott
American, 1907-2003
The Gleaners, 1936
Oil on canvas
28" x 40 1/4" (71.1 cm x 102.2 cm)
Signed and dated: lower left
Gift of Evelyne and Burton Callicott 94.7

Burton Callicott was born in Terre Haute, Indiana, and moved to Memphis at the age of four. Encouraged by his stepfather, Callicott studied portrait painting at the Cleveland School of Art, graduating in 1931. Returning to Memphis, he taught at the Memphis College of Art from 1937 to 1973. Callicott was selected in 1934 as one of ten Tennessee artists to participate in the federally funded Public Works of Art Project, for which he painted a three-panel mural in Memphis' Pink Palace Museum depicting the Spanish conquistador Hernando de Soto. While the artist soon moved away from figuration, he did complete a small number of significant figural compositions during the 1930s. Inspired by Mexican muralist Diego Rivera and American Regionalist painter Thomas Hart Benton (see page 180), and their interest in the common man, Callicott painted *The Gleaners* in 1936, which was selected to represent Tennessee at the World's Fair in New York City in 1939.

The Gleaners depicts three African Americans collecting coal that was dropped from passing trains. Callicott, who recalled seeing the poor with their gunnysacks and pails as he walked his wife to work each day, had a deeply sympathetic response to their plight. The foragers are depicted in torn clothing and with swollen knuckles and worn facial expressions. Even the two small dogs waiting for their masters are emaciated and tired. The bent posture of the figures is echoed in the curved diagonal line of the railroad tracks, which are lined with commercial structures. The tracks lead the viewer to the store in the background marked "COAL," where the gleaners will sell what they collect. The muted reds, greens, blues, and browns contribute to the somber mood of the painting, yet through the figures' large size, Callicott imbues them with monumentality. This image of determination and perseverance is a moving portrayal of strength in the face of adversity during the Great Depression.

KHD

Georgia O'Keeffe
American, 1887-1986
Waterfall—No.1— Iao Valley—Maui, 1939
Oil on canvas
19 1/2" x 16" (48.6 cm x 40.6 cm)
Signed: back
Gift of Art Today 76.7

Along with the other artists in the circle of photographer and gallerist Alfred Stieglitz, Georgia O'Keeffe was intent on developing a new American painting that was aware of European Modernism, but that reflected contemporary American culture. Through abstraction—the use of heightened and arbitrary color, simplification of form, and distortion—these artists explored industrialization, commerce, and the natural American landscape.

In 1929, O'Keeffe began painting New Mexico. It was an important moment that signaled a change in her subject matter, away from flowers and cityscapes, and toward an emphasis on the landscape of the Southwest. This change, however, was also an attempt to circumvent the Freudian readings of her images, and offered a larger framework for exploring Americanness. In Hawaii, O'Keeffe found many of the same features she admired in the desert landscapes of New Mexico.

Dole Pineapple Company hired O'Keeffe in 1939 to produce two images to be used for advertising. She spent more than two months traveling in Hawaii and completed twenty paintings. Some, including the two that were featured in Dole ads in *Vogue* and *The Saturday Evening Post*, were not completed until after her return to New York.[1] *Waterfall—No.1* is the first of three versions of the Iao Valley, Maui, a place sacred to Hawaiians. The image continues her interest in indigenous religions, evidenced in her earlier works of pueblo churches. The smoky cloud hanging in the upper valley evokes an ethereal quality suggesting a primeval and holy place. As is typical of her style, O'Keeffe brings the landscape to the surface of the canvas, filling the space. Nature is transformed—smoothed out, monumentalized, and flattened into large simplified forms painted in a reduced palette. The light green to the sides frames the darker green of the center, pulling one's eye into the verdant distance. The waterfall is evoked through a simplified gray white line of paint that appears and reappears as it moves through the valley. More than a subjective interpretation of objects and nature, O'Keeffe's landscape evokes a timelessness that transcends actual location or objects depicted.

MP

[1]Jennifer Saville, *Georgia O'Keeffe: Paintings of Hawaii* (Honolulu: Honolulu Academy of Arts, 1990), pp. 17-18.

Jack Levine
American, b. 1915
City Lights, 1940
Oil on canvas
54" x 36" (137.2 cm x 91.4 cm)
Signed: lower right
Gift of Edith and Milton Lowenthal 78.6

Jack Levine's parents were Lithuanian Jews who immigrated to Boston before the turn of the 20th century. Showing early promise, he began art classes at age eight, studying at the Boston Museum of Fine Arts Saturday School and the West End Community Center. His early training emphasized the work of Diego Velázquez, El Greco, Francisco de Goya (represented in the Brooks Collection), and Peter Paul Rubens, as well as modern Expressionist painters such as Georges Rouault and Chaim Soutine (see page 122). Imaginative drawing, or re-creating from memory what he had observed, was encouraged by his teachers along with a thorough understanding of color theory. After participating periodically in the Easel Division of the Works Progress Administration Federal Art Project in the 1930s, he was drafted by the army in 1942, and toward the end of World War II was transferred to New York City. By then he was known as a Social Realist who satirically explored political corruption and human foibles through a painterly Expressionist style.

City Lights was painted in response to the death of Levine's father in 1939. An eerie night scene, the painting is lit not by the stars, but by the artificial lights of the city. The constricted, shallow space is filled with objects conjured through jagged, slashing brushstrokes. Three suited men, who are working class like Levine's father, are positioned in a semicircle, standing on a section of a brick street. Characteristic of Levine's figures, they are short with large heads. Emphasis is placed on their fleshy, thickly painted faces, which provide a living contrast with the ethereal skull above them. The empty sockets of the skeleton are aligned with the eyes of the figure below, a link between the living and the dead that instigates a macabre dialogue between the viewer and the painting. Overall, the impression created is bleak, grim, and threatening.

MP

Reginald Marsh
American (b. France), 1898-1954
Dead Man's Curve, 1940
Ink and watercolor
26 1/2 " x 39 3/4 " (67.3 cm x 100.9 cm)
Signed and dated: lower right
Eugenia Buxton Whitnel Fund 73.17

Born in Paris to American parents, Reginald Marsh grew up in New Jersey and New York. After graduating from Yale University, he returned to New York and attended the Arts Students League, worked for *The New Yorker,* and served as a wartime correspondent for *Life* magazine. His experiences as an illustrator trained him to sketch events and people quickly and accurately, and he later developed his sketches into larger, more detailed images. It was Marsh's ambition to capture the vibrant energy of New York City in visual form; he incessantly searched the streets, subways, beaches, and burlesque shows for scenes and subjects that embodied the city's character and vitality. His depictions of the urban landscape were rendered in murals, paintings, drawings, etchings, lithographs, and photographs.

Full of pedestrians and traffic, the watercolor captures the sensations of the hustle and bustle of New York City. Bursting with energy and movement, *Dead Man's Curve* is typical of the artist's work in its multifigured composition and sinuous, rhythmic lines. Voluptuous ladies with their flowing skirts strut nonchalantly in front of a Mack truck, personifying the sensory excitement of the congested metropolitan streets. The artist often chose to depict the working class, like these females, creating visual metaphors for the raw energy of the American populace. A new sector of the American workforce has been captured in this 1940s image. With many men overseas during World War II, women came to play considerable roles in the urban workplace. Marsh's work is a testament to his fascination with and affinity for the contemporary city life of his day.

KVG

William Edmondson
American, 1874-1951
Courting Lady, ca. 1940s
Limestone
15 1/2" x 5 7/8" x 8" (39.4 cm x 14.9 cm x 20.3 cm)
Gift of AutoZone, Inc. 2001.15.13

William Edmondson's parents were former slaves who supported themselves by sharecropping in Davidson County, Tennessee, although by 1907 the family had settled in Nashville. Edmondson, who worked as a janitor at the Woman's Hospital, purchased the lot next door to his house and planted fruit trees and a garden. Here, in 1931, he set up his studio and commenced his extraordinary body of work.

A vision of God inspired Edmondson's carving. He stated, "I was out in my driveway with some pieces of stone when I heard a voice telling me to pick up my tools and start to work on a tombstone. I looked up in the sky and right there in the noon daylight He hung a tombstone out for me to make."[1] With a railroad spike and hammer, Edmondson embarked on a prolific career as a carver of "tombstones and garden ornaments," as the sign on his studio advertised.

Edmondson carved many images of little ladies. The face of *Courting Lady*, like that of all of his figures, has generic features that do not appear to reference a specific race or person. Generally, the ladies are dressed in old-fashioned, floor-length dresses. This lady (one of two Edmondson sculptures AutoZone donated to the Brooks Collection) lifts her skirt, exposing her slip to attract a suitor. Her slip, with its smooth surface and zigzag hem, is differentiated from the dress, which has deeply carved grooves representing a fabric pattern. The head of the flat chisel he used is readily visible in the dress, where the path of each hammer blow can be seen. And, as is also typical of his work, attention has been lavished on her large bun.

Although Alfred H. Barr Jr. gave Edmondson a solo exhibition at the Museum of Modern Art in 1937, his work was shown infrequently during his lifetime. Since the 1970s, however, his sculpture has been exhibited with increasing frequency in both solo and group exhibitions.

MP

[1] John Thompson, *Nashville Tennessean*, February 9, 1941.

Raphael Soyer
American (b. Russia), 1899-1987
Two Bit Suzzle, ca. 1940
Oil on canvas
9 1/2" x 11 3/8" (24.1cm x 28.9 cm)
Signed: top right
Gift of Howard Foote 2003.10.5

Raphael Soyer was born in Russia and immigrated to the United States shortly before World War I with his artist brothers Isaac (see page 178) and Moses (represented in the Brooks Collection). Starting art classes at a young age, he attended Cooper Union from 1914 to 1917 and the National Academy of Design from 1918 to 1922, and studied intermittently at the Art Students League from 1920 to 1926. During the 1930s, he was employed by the Works Progress Administration, and was a member of such political groups as the John Reed Club, a communist organization, and the American Artists' Congress. Like his brothers, he was a Social Realist who depicted the difficulty of urban life during the Great Depression, often painting sympathetic images of the homeless and unemployed. Soyer also painted many images of his family, artist friends, dancers, bohemians, and especially women. Consistently working from models, he depicted nudes or partially clothed figures in compositions ranging from quiet interior group scenes to solitary female figures.

A small painting of an intimate scene, *Two Bit Suzzle* is also a study of a hard-boiled workingwoman. The location is easily identified, as Soyer repeatedly painted his studio, which, whether peopled by fellow artists or models, included his easel, chairs, and a screen behind which the models could disrobe. Here, the woman appears to be taking a break from her duties with a cigarette in a holder dangling from her red lips. Behind her, loosely painted, her clothes hang from the screen. Interested not solely in the female form, Soyer attempted to convey something of the personalities of his sitters. Seated at an angle with her shoulders back, sizing up the viewer out of the corners of her eyes, she appears self-assured, almost confrontational, and comfortable with her state of undress. She may be louche, her time only worth twenty-five cents, but she is a force to be reckoned with.

MP

Ansel Easton Adams
American, 1902-1984
Moonrise, Hernandez, New Mexico, 1941
Silver gelatin print
15 1/2" x 19 1/4" (39.4 cm x 48.9 cm)
Signed: mount lower right
Gift of Art Today 77.9

When he was fourteen years old, Ansel Adams took his Brownie box camera to the Yosemite Valley and began his lifelong interest in landscape photography. While documenting specific locations, he also hoped to reveal, in the tradition of Ralph Waldo Emerson and Walt Whitman, the spirituality within nature. He started working for the Sierra Club in 1920, becoming its official photographer by 1928. Trained as a musician, Adams supported himself playing concerts and teaching until 1930, when he turned his attention full-time to photography.

While working as a photomuralist for the Department of the Interior in 1941, Adams shot *Moonrise, Hernandez, New Mexico* as part of an assignment to create a series of portraits of different regions of the country. Although signs of humanity are evident in the pueblo church, cemetery, and scattered buildings in the foreground, they are dwarfed by nature; over half of the image is the night sky with the moon hanging slightly off center. Adams developed what he termed the zone system to control the tonal range from dark to light with a high degree of precision. The photograph reads as alternating bands of dark and light, beginning at the bottom with the stretch of desert shrubs in shadow, followed by the highlighted buildings, and on up through the landscape into the sky. The pure white ribbon of clouds and the moon, thrown into stark relief by the inky sky, vie for the viewer's attention with the highlighted crosses and tombstones. Reinforced by the sharp focus, the image conveys the photographer's awe before the sublimity of nature—his rumination on humanity's insignificance before natural forces.

Throughout his career, Adams devoted himself to promoting nature and photography. His breathtaking photographs of remote areas of national parks increased awareness of conservation and preservation efforts. Through exhibitions, publications, and related efforts—including cofounding both the Department of Photography at the Museum of Modern Art in 1940 and the magazine *Aperture* in 1952—he brought greater critical recognition to the art of photography, while increasing its popularity.

MP

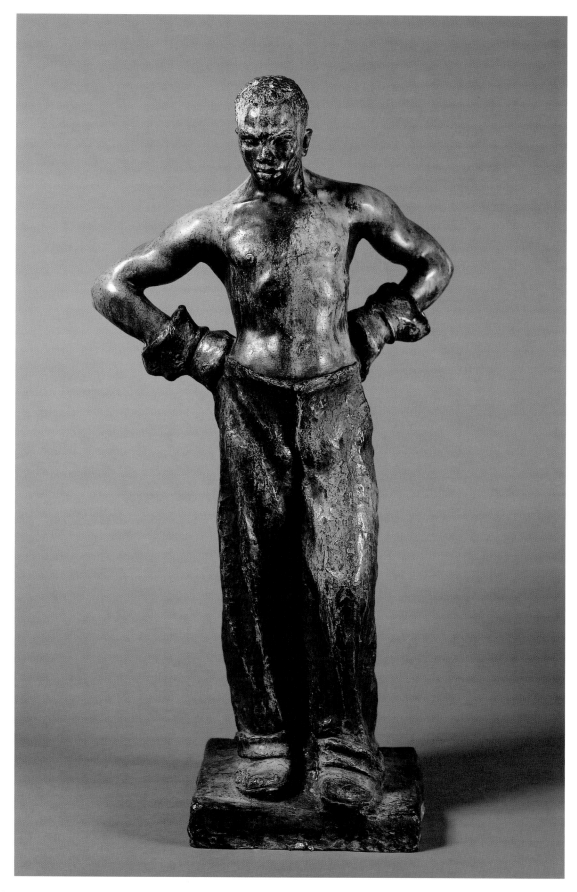

Leon Koury
American, 1909-1993
Compress Worker, 1941
Bronze
44" x 23" x 11 1/4" (111.8 cm x 58.4 cm x 28.6 cm)
Gift of the Brooks Art Gallery League 41.6

Compress workers move bales of cotton weighing between 500 and 600 pounds. As a result, they are physically fit with superb muscle definition. For Leon Koury, who sculpted the human figure, they provided a perfect model of a heroic male body. Rejecting abstraction in favor of naturalism, Koury sought to update the classical tradition. Conceived in the form of a Greek kouros, with weight thrown back on his right hip and his left leg bent, the *Compress Worker* is celebrated as an industrial laborer rather than as an athlete or a god.

Although the *Compress Worker* is captured at a moment of rest, the figure is anything but static, with his arms akimbo, head turned down at an angle, and torso arced back slightly. Every limb is subtly jutting, bending, or turning—emphasizing the three-dimensionality of the figure while conveying, even though checked at this moment, his energy and strength. Not merely an exercise in anatomy, the various surfaces are beautifully differentiated, from the smooth skin to the rough fabric of the pants and the texture of the hair. Attention is lavished also on small details that individualize the figure, such as the worn right shoe that exposes his toes. The pose and details combine to create a sympathetic portrait of a dignified person whose job is physical and challenging.

After high school, Koury moved to New York City and became a studio assistant to sculptor Malvina Hoffman. He learned how to cast clay working for New Jersey ceramic companies. When his mother died, he returned to Greenville, Mississippi, to take care of his father and did not leave again. Opening first a nightclub in his father's defunct grocery store, he later installed a studio, taught art classes, and completed portraits of his Delta neighbors, as well as commissioned busts of local luminaries William Faulkner and Hodding Carter. Although little known today, Koury exhibited at the 1939 World's Fair, the Whitney Museum of American Art, and both New York and West Coast galleries.

MP

MODERN ART
1945-2004

AP II/IV   E Catlett 1946

In Harriet Tubman I helped hundreds to freedom.

Elizabeth Catlett
American, b. 1915
***In Harriet Tubman I helped hundreds to freedom* from the series
The Negro Woman, 1946-1947**
Linocut, AP II/IV
9 1/8" x 7" (23.2 cm x 17.8 cm)
Signed and dated: lower right
Gift of AutoZone, Inc. 2001.15.1I

Born in Washington, D.C., Elizabeth Catlett graduated in 1937 from Howard University, where she became acquainted with African art and the work of Mexican muralists such as Diego Rivera. She received an MFA degree in sculpture from the University of Iowa in 1940. Grant Wood, with whom she studied in Iowa, urged Catlett to make art about what she knew best, which for her was the African American experience. After a visit to Mexico in 1946, she established permanent residence in Mexico City in 1947.

Motivated by the socialist ideals of a world free of class oppression and racial injustice, many African American artists—such as Hale Woodruff, Charles White, Samella Sanders Lewis, and John Biggers—followed the example of the Mexican muralists. In their art they expressed a sense of pride in their African American heritage and identity, and they, like Catlett, were inspired by the social commitment, accessible style, subject matter, and choice of media of the Mexican muralists. Prints were a logical medium because they were inexpensive, could be mass-produced, and, therefore, could be widely disseminated. Working in the Taller de Gráfica Popular (Popular Graphics Workshop), Catlett adopted the strategy of artists working there—creating an art for the people that conveyed a conscious political strategy, celebrated courageous acts, and depicted the tragic martyrdom of ordinary workers.

In her first major work at the Taller, a series of fifteen linocuts titled *The Negro Woman* (the Brooks owns the complete series), Catlett created small, powerful prints depicting the historic oppression, resistance, and survival of African American women. Before the Civil War, Harriet Tubman had fled slavery and then, for more than a decade, led runaway slaves to freedom in the North. Tubman is depicted in monumental scale towering over the weary travelers who, under the protection and guidance of her extended arm, carry their babies and worldly possessions to a life free from bondage. The thickly incised lines of her dress, arms, and face create energetic swirls of movement as they are repeated in the clothing of the background figures. *In Harriet Tubman I helped hundreds to freedom* is a dynamic image, revealing the passion and courage of its heroine.

KVG

Walt Kuhn
American, 1880-1949
Clown with Red Tights, 1948
Oil on canvas
30 5/8" x 24 5/8" (77.8 cm x 62.6 cm)
Signed and dated: lower left
Eugenia Buxton Whitnel Funds 73.15

William "Walt" Kuhn was born in New York, studied at the Brooklyn Polytechnic Institute, and began his career as a cartoonist and illustrator. He served as one of the organizers of the 1913 New York *Armory Show*, which showcased the vanguard of European painting and sculpture. The exhibit influenced a distinct change in Kuhn's artistic style; his paintings began to demonstrate Henri Matisse's arbitrary use of bold colors. Kuhn developed a loose, fluid style and began to incorporate broad, simplified forms into his compositions.

In the 1920s he became immersed in show business, which shaped his mature life as an artist. As illustrated in *Clown with Red Tights*, he began painting theatrical genre portraits, including clowns, acrobats, showgirls, and other thespians. Viewing the circus and vaudeville as microcosms of the world, he referred to his subjects as metaphors of society. His works usually portray the overworked and underpaid anonymous working-class participants of show business, rather than the stars of the stage. Subjects are rarely depicted in action; instead they appear in isolated portrait settings as if posing before or after a performance. Like many of Kuhn's other sitters, the clown is positioned frontally against a somber backdrop, which creates a mood of physical and emotional alienation. The figure appears enervated, and his expression is sad and devoid of humor. While the vibrant red leotard evokes the joviality and energy associated with jesters, the clown's pensive stare suggests feelings of loneliness and depression. Accentuating his tired eyes, the white facial makeup further emphasizes his melancholic mood. *Clown with Red Tights* typifies Kuhn's empathetic twenty-year relationship with nameless circus and stage performers.

KVG

Jacques Lipchitz
French (b. Lithuania), 1891-1973
Sacrifice III, 1949-1957
Bronze
54 1/2" x 38" x 25 1/2" (138.4 cm x 96.5 cm x 64.8 cm)
Signed: verso lower right
Eugenia Buxton Whitnel Funds 74.27

Jacques Lipchitz was born in Druskieniki, Lithuania, and immigrated to Paris in 1909 to pursue his interest in art. He studied at the École des Beaux-Arts and the Académie Julian, and became friends with Cubist painters Pablo Picasso and Juan Gris. The influence of these important artists is evident in Lipchitz's early sculptures of musicians, harlequins, and still lifes, created in a Cubist style. During the 1930s, his work became more symbolic, expressive, and highly personal, often relating to events in the artist's own life. Though still abstract in form, his work moved toward more naturalistic, recognizable subjects, including scenes from mythology, biblical stories, and contemporary historical events such as World War II. In 1941, with little more than a portfolio of drawings in his possession, Lipchitz fled the Nazis and set up a studio in New York.

As a Jew, Lipchitz was drawn to subjects from the Old Testament. Also concerned about the fate of the Jewish people and pondering the birth of the new state of Israel in 1948, the artist began to explore the idea of sacrifice. *Sacrifice III* depicts a man wearing the ceremonial tallith (prayer shawl) while grasping a rooster around the throat with one large hand and thrusting the pronounced dagger into the rooster's chest with the other. Modeled with a rough, nodular texture, the sculpture is comprised of voluminous, abstracted forms. The figure stands firmly, with his bare feet slightly apart and his stylized robe open to reveal his muscular body. Intensifying the dramatic moment, the rooster flails wildly—his beak open wide, wings extended, and talons attacking the figure. The lamb, traditionally a Christian rather than a Judaic symbol, peers quietly from between the man's legs and may represent the innocents who are saved and whose future will be secured as a result of the sacrifice.

KHD

Jackson Pollock
American, 1912-1956
Number 9, 1951
Silk screen 19/25 (O'Conner/Thaw)
19" x 16 3/4" (48.3 cm x 42.6 cm)
Signed and dated: lower left
Gift of Art Today 57.10

Jackson Pollock was raised in Wyoming and California, and the grandeur of the expansive landscape and intense, individualist sensibility of the American West left a lifelong impression on him. Pollock's mentor, Regionalist painter Thomas Hart Benton (see page 180), encouraged him to create a style that was unique to the United States. While Pollock embraced Benton's search to define an American artistic style, he eventually rejected Benton's emphasis on rural American subjects in favor of a more spontaneous and unconscious approach influenced by Surrealism. By the mid-20th century Pollock was a pivotal figure of Abstract Expressionism, which was the first American art movement to affect international art.

Number 9, is one of six prints from a portfolio (the Brooks Collection includes the complete portfolio) that Pollock made with the assistance of his brother, Sanford McCoy, a master printer. The prints are exact renditions of black paintings and drawings that were exhibited in 1951 at the Betty Parsons Gallery. High-quality photographs were taken of the work in the exhibition and the negatives were transferred onto photosensitive screens from which silk screens were printed. The monochromatic series illustrates Pollock's trademark process of paint poured and dripped from sticks and hardened brushes. Through this method, he created thick black pools that progressively shifted into thin threads of paint. Here, the composition oscillates between figuration and abstraction with a recognizable image of a face materializing on the left side of the print. Pollock claimed that the stream of consciousness naturally fluctuates from representation to abstraction as a result of working immediately and directly from the unconscious.

AV

Ernest Withers
American, b. 1922
Jazz Stroll Down Beale Street, Cotton Makers' Jubilee, 1952
Silver gelatin print, toned
10" x 10 3/8" (25.4 cm x 26.2 cm)
Memphis Brooks Museum of Art Purchase 86.31.1

Ernest Withers is well known for his iconic images of the civil rights movement, among them Emmett Till's funeral, the sanitation workers' strike in Memphis in 1968, and Dr. Martin Luther King Jr.'s assassination. He brought the same compositional skills and keen eye for telling detail to his photographs of African American life in Memphis.

A native Memphian, Withers' earliest shots documented events at Manassas High School, where he was a student. It was not until he entered the army during World War II, however, that he received formal training. When it was determined that his regiment did not need a photographer, Withers set up a darkroom so that during his off-hours he could take pictures for soldiers to send home to their families. Upon his return, he set up a series of studios around Memphis and has been making photographs ever since. His subjects are many: nightclubs, debutantes, funerals, weddings, Sunday school classes, insurance work, Negro Baseball League players and teams, and musicians such as B.B. King, Aretha Franklin, Elvis Presley, and Isaac Hayes.

This joyous image of the Cotton Makers' Jubilee (today known as the Memphis Kemet Jubilee) documents an important social event. As African Americans were allowed limited participation in the Cotton Carnival, the Jubilee was started as a separate event in 1936.[1] Over the years, it expanded to include a series of programs, including a ball, three parades, and the Spirit of Cotton contest, a pageant for African American college women from southern states. *Jazz Stroll Down Beale Street, Cotton Makers' Jubilee* celebrates the vibrant performance of these young women strutting down Beale Street, then the heart of the African American district in Memphis, while eager crowds line the street to watch the parade. In their light outfits, the strollers are dramatically set off against the nighttime setting. Their skirts—decorated with musical notes—swirl around them creating a pattern across the print. The highlighted street line emphasizes the dynamic diagonal composition. A microcosm of its time, the photograph captures the fashions, music, and culture of Withers' community.

MP

Charles Burchfield
American, 1893-1967
September Sunshine, 1956
Watercolor and pencil
39 7/8" x 29 7/8" (101.3 cm x 76 cm)
Signed: lower left
Gift of Art Today 63.2

After studying at the Cleveland Institute of Art from 1912 to 1916, and at the National Academy of Design for one day, Charles Burchfield moved to Salem, Ohio, where he worked at a factory and painted during his lunch hour and on weekends. His small early watercolors abstractly presented nature and various emotional states, such as melancholy and fear. Moving to Buffalo, New York, in 1921, he was employed as a wallpaper designer until 1929, when he devoted himself to painting full-time. From 1929 to 1943, his watercolors abandoned fantasy to capture urban subjects in a larger scale and a more realistic style.

September Sunshine is characteristic of Burchfield's late Expressionist phase in which he created ecstatic images of nature. Abstracted to simplified repeating patterns, the plant forms are nonetheless recognizable as shrubs and trees. The vitality of nature is suggested through the zigzagging forms that explode with life; one can almost hear the breeze sighing through the trees and the sound of crickets hiding in the long grass. A pantheist in the tradition of Ralph Waldo Emerson, Burchfield also attempted to convey the spirituality he saw in nature. Here, the central tree is surrounded by a yellow halo that evokes a mystical or ecstatic state that is underscored by the parallel lines of yellow dots climbing up into the heavens. Humanity's place in this idyllic scene is represented by the church spire and house roof on either side of the watercolor. Both structures, however, are dwarfed by the landscape that envelopes them.

MP

Josef Albers
American (b. German), 1888-1976
Study for Homage to the Square: Young Voice, 1957
Oil on Masonite board
24" x 24" (61 cm x 61 cm)
Signed and dated: lower right
Gift of Art Today 60.38

Josef Albers is recognized as an artist and an educator. Born into a family of artisans and carpenters, he was exposed to a tradition of careful and precise workmanship that influenced his later endeavors. After studying and then lecturing at the Bauhaus in Germany, Albers immigrated to the United States in the early 1930s, as did many German artists fleeing the Nazis. Once in the States, Albers taught at Black Mountain College in North Carolina before moving to Yale University, where he became chairman of the Fine Art Department. Focusing on color theory, his teachings introduced not only basic design, but also principles of color and perception. Through his own work, Albers investigated and illustrated formal relationships based on color combinations, variations in saturation, and optical illusions. He published his ideas in *The Interaction of Color,* an influential book that outlines the visual, perceptual, and psychological characteristics of color.

In 1950 Albers began painting the *Homage to the Square* series, on which he worked until his death in 1976. The *Homage* cycle used the square as its basic element because the form provided a simple, repeatable geometric shape that then freed him to focus on color relationships. Albers' process was just as simple as his compositional vocabulary. Using a limited amount of paint, he created impeccably uniform surfaces. For example, in *Study for Homage to the Square: Young Voice,* a large painted square serves as the background upon which three more squares of diminishing sizes and varying shades are placed. These contrasts combine to suggest spatial depth and visual vibration within the painting.

AV

Walter I. Anderson
American, 1903-1965
Lagoons—Horn Island, ca. 1960
Watercolor over pencil
8 1/2" x 11" (21.6 cm x 27.9 cm)
Brooks Memorial Art Gallery Purchase; funds provided by the Memphis Park
Commission, the Brooks Fine Arts Foundation, and Mrs. Walter I. Anderson
69.7.9

Born in New Orleans, Louisiana, Walter I. Anderson attended Parsons School of
Design and the Pennsylvania Academy of Fine Arts. Like many artists and writers, he
was drawn back to the South, which served as an inspiration for his art. Many artistic
styles influenced him, including ancient and primitive art, Art Nouveau, Art Deco,
and American landscape painting. Aldolpho Best-Maugard's *Method for Creative
Design*, however, had the most lasting effect on his work. This treatise reduced all of
art into seven geometric patterns and these forms dominate much of Anderson's
artwork. He was an astonishingly prolific artist who worked in a variety of media,
including oil, watercolor, wood, printmaking, textiles, and ceramics. The Brooks
Collection includes examples of his work in all of these media.

Anderson believed man and nature had a symbiotic relationship—man needed the
natural world in order to achieve spiritual enlightenment, while nature required the
artist to fully "realize" the significance of its forms. It was the process of creation that
consumed him, rather than the final product. Over an eighteen-year period he
braved the elements and made lone voyages to his sanctuary on Horn Island, an
uninhabited barrier island off the Mississippi Gulf Coast. Living as one with his
environment, he recorded the island's landscape, flora, and fauna in sketches and
watercolors.

Among the subjects he painted numerous times and in various seasons were the
island's lagoons. Here he depicts one inlet at the height of summer with the lush
greens and yellows of the foliage and the brilliant blues of the sea and sky. It is low
tide and the artist uses various hues of purple for the sand, shells, and rocks revealed
by the receding waters. Red-winged blackbirds perch on stalks of sea grass, while a
pair of terns fly overhead. The repetition of shapes and motifs, such as the wave-like
arcs of vegetation, unifies the composition and creates an overall decorative
pattern, which is characteristic of much of the artist's work.

KVG

Ben Shahn

American (b. Lithuania), 1898-1969

***Mural Study for Tree of Life*, commissioned for the transatlantic ship *Shalom*, 1963**

Tempera on board

18 1/8"x 85 1/2" (46 cm x 217.2 cm)

Signed: lower right

Eugenia Buxton Whitnel Funds 73.16

TO THE REMEMBRANCE OF GOD BY THE ART OF PHEIDIAS AN EGYPTIAN BY PAYING

iR DIVERGENCES: ONLY LET THEM KNOW. LET THEM LOVE: LET THEM REMEMBER

Immigrating to New York with his family in 1906, Ben Shahn apprenticed with a lithographer from 1913 to 1917, and later studied at the National Academy of Design and the Art Students League. Traveling twice to Europe between 1924 and 1929, Shahn studied the old masters as well as paintings by Raoul Dufy, Henri Matisse, Pablo Picasso, and Paul Klee. When he determined, however, that he wanted to tell stories through his paintings, Shahn developed a simplified representational style. He is known best for his paintings of the trial and execution of the working-class anarchists Nicola Sacco and Bartolomeo Vanzetti, in which Shahn excoriated the New England aristocrats who perpetrated what he saw as a grave social injustice. During the 1930s and 1940s, he shot photographs for the Farm Services Administration and painted for the Public Works of Art Project. After World War II, he began painting allegorical and biblical imagery based on a complex personal iconography.

Tree of Life is the final study for a mosaic mural (today in the collection of the New Jersey State Museum) commissioned for the passenger ship SS *Shalom*, a transatlantic passenger ship owned by The American Israeli Shipping Company. A paean to religious and aesthetic tolerance, the mural is also a rumination on the need to link science with philosophy. Bordering the bottom and top are the words of Maximus of Tyre, a 2nd-century Greek philosopher who advocated freedom of religion and respect for visual imagery that facilitated the practice of religion. In the center is a figure who can be interpreted either as three individuals or as three facets of a unified being. A philosopher reads the Aramaic text in front of him: "Where the book is, the sword is not." To the left, he is framed by a botanist who holds a thorny plant with blood red roots resembling a human heart. To the right, a physicist clasps a molecular model.[1] The sides of the image are balanced through more molecular models and stellar constellations that tie *Tree of Life* to its companion mosaic, *Atomic Table*. After World War II Shahn worried about the threat of nuclear technology; here he celebrates the unification of science with the spiritual.

MP

[1] Frances K. Pohl, *Ben Shahn* (San Francisco: Pomegranate Artbooks, 1993), p. 29.

Carroll Cloar
American, 1918-1993
Where the Southern Cross the Yellow Dog, 1965
Casein tempera on Masonite
23" x 33 3/4" (58.4 cm x 85.7 cm)
Signed: lower left
Brooks Fine Arts Foundation Purchase 65.17

Born in Earle, Arkansas, Carroll Cloar attended the Memphis Academy of Arts (today Memphis College of Art), and graduated from Southwestern University (today Rhodes College) in Memphis. Later he traveled to Europe, Asia, and Mexico, but he was always drawn back to the South. Like many southerners, he was a storyteller, poetically rendering memories, fantasies, feelings, and dreams into visual form. His works capture moments frozen in time that represent a nostalgia for rural southern life. In this painting, the artist brings visual form to a blues song. The title comes from W.C. Handy's 1914 tune *The Yellow Dog Blues*, whose final line is "he's gone where the Southern cross the Yellow Dog." This crossing in Moorhead, Mississippi, known colloquially as the Yellow Dog, was where the Southern Railroad line and the Yazoo and Mississippi Valley Railroad line once intersected.

Prominently placed at the center of the painting are the horizontal and vertical lines of the railroad crossing. Walking along the tracks are an African American man and woman, whose flattened forms are static and fixed. The linear perspective created through the diminishing rail tracks, road, buildings, and power poles leads the viewer's eye into the distance, bringing to mind the many miles of track and numerous towns ahead. These linear qualities are repeated in the diagonal blades of grass, which are juxtaposed with the rounded forms of the trees and woods. The artist painted with casein tempera, a medium characterized by dry, smooth surfaces, yet through his application of paint Cloar achieved a rich sense of texture. By repeating small dots of colors in the leaves of the trees, he created the vibrant foliage of an autumn day. The cool blue of the Mississippi sky is contrasted by the warm hues of gold and orange that highlight the rest of the painting. Through his use of color, he unifies the composition while simultaneously capturing the dryness and heat of a sunbaked southern day. The work refers to a specific time and place, but like many of Cloar's artworks, the scene could be in any small American town.

KVG

Roy Lichtenstein
American, 1923-1997
Sweet Dreams, Baby! from the portfolio *11 Pop Artists, vol. II,* 1965
Silk screen 137/200
27" x 23" (68.6 cm x 58.4 cm)
Signed: lower right
Joint purchase of the Memphis Park Commission and Brooks Fine Arts
Foundation 65.116

Pop artist Roy Lichtenstein was known for his paintings, prints, and installations that recontextualized imagery from mass culture. Reacting against Abstract Expressionism, Pop artists favored an objective approach to painting that was emotionally detached and removed evidence of the artist's hand from the work of art. Extracting images from popular culture and reconfiguring them into his work, Lichtenstein narrowed the distinction between fine and popular art. He adopted comic book imagery replicating the process and look of manufactured printed pulp through benday dots, vivid primary hues, text, speech balloons, and thick black lines.

By cropping and removing parts of the original comic strip composition, Lichtenstein was able to establish formal relationships based on balance and color. His controlled art-making process is often juxtaposed with an expressive or emotional moment; for example, aggression is overtly displayed in *Sweet Dreams, Baby!* Although the scene is comprised of two partial figures, the image captures a dynamic and violent moment. One man's punch, dramatically emphasized through arcing motion lines and the vibrant "POW!" in bright red capitals, knocks the other man's head out of the frame. The narrative sequence is suspended—it is unclear what led to the altercation or what will occur next. Lichtenstein's title offers an interesting double meaning, as "sweet dreams, baby" is traditionally an endearing phrase. In this particular context, however, it suggests a "farewell" to the man who was just hit.

AV

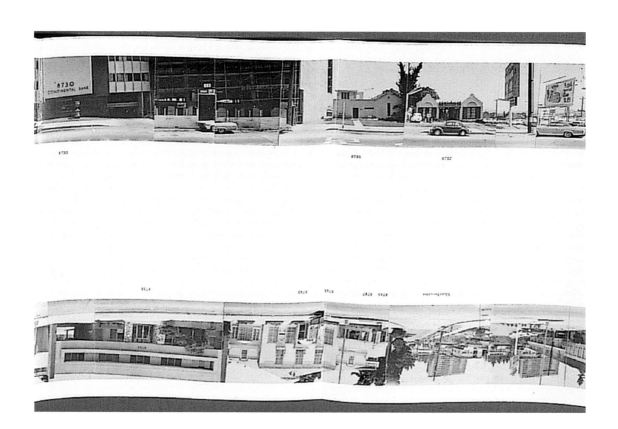

Edward Ruscha
American, b. 1937
Every Building on the Sunset Strip, 1966
Self-published, Los Angeles, first edition of 1,000
Photolithographic concertina
7 1/8" x 5 7/8" (18.1 cm x 14.6 cm)
Gift of the Isabel Ehrlich Goodman and Charles F. Goodman Collection
90.19.19a,b

Ed Ruscha produced twenty photographic books between 1963 and 1978, of which *Every Building on the Sunset Strip* is the most famous. As the title suggests, every building on both sides of Los Angeles' famous Sunset Strip was photographed and the images were hand pasted into an accordion-like book, unfolding as a single sheet measuring nearly 27 feet in length. Shot sequentially in real time with a motorized Nikon camera mounted on the back of a moving pickup truck, the resulting montage creates an almost cinematic flow documenting the vernacular architecture of Hollywood in 1966.

Ruscha's interest in mass culture derives from his time at the prestigious Chouinard Art Institute in Los Angeles from 1956 to 1960 (which became CalArts in 1961). First studying commercial art cartooning, he soon turned to fine art, but continued to borrow source imagery from print advertising and billboard design. His paintings featuring product logos and hard-edged depictions of roadside gas stations were influential in the early days of the Pop Art movement and remain so to this day. Like many artists of the era, Ruscha did not limit himself to a single medium. Instead, he frequently crossed between printmaking, painting, drawing, and photographic books, often expressing his trademark deadpan wit.

This seminal work reflects Ruscha's fascination with the driving culture of Los Angeles and the city that spawned it. Rather than focusing on the custom cars that maneuvered the city's streets, as did his fellow artists Billy Al Bengston and Craig Kauffman, Ruscha was drawn to the experience of the ride itself and the flood of ephemeral street iconography it presented.[1] The book's layout mimics that of the boulevard itself, with buildings facing each other across a white median of blank page as cars appear to drive in opposite directions. Instead of idealizing buildings as individual monuments of special significance, this orientation provides the viewer with an unfolding narrative that documents the act of vehicular movement through the landscape.

JW

[1]Neal Benezra and Kerry Brougher, *Ed Ruscha* (Washington, D.C.: Hirshhorn Museum, Smithsonian Institution, 2000), p. 159.

George Rickey
American, 1907-2002
Two Lines Oblique No. 7, ca. 1968
Stainless steel
300" x 25" (762 cm x 63.5 cm)
Gift of Art Today 73.7

Born in Indiana and raised in Scotland, George Rickey studied history and painting in England and France. During World War II he worked as a gunnery instructor in the army. It was this experience that prompted his interest in combining science and technology with art, particularly through sculpture. Having access to a machine workshop while in the army, Rickey created his first small sculptures, and by 1948 he had abandoned painting altogether. Intrigued and influenced by Alexander Calder's mobiles and the abstract geometric forms of early-20th-century Constructivism, a movement that linked art with industry and technology, Rickey created structures that respond to the slightest movement of air.

The Brooks' outdoor sculpture exemplifies Rickey's mature style of large, reductive, geometric forms created of stainless steel. Combining engineering principles with the unpredictability of nature, Rickey created sculptures that are stable and geometrically ordered, but are simultaneously vulnerable to the weather's changing conditions. Two Lines Oblique No. 7 is a vertical structure that branches into two arms, each connected at the apex to a spear-like length of steel. Rotating on precision ball bearings that were developed by Rickey, the blades are delicately balanced and oscillate with the air's irregular rhythm. The large, linear, and slender Two Lines Oblique No. 7 harmonizes with its environment. Although the sculpture is made from industrial materials, its presence is graceful, sleek, and quiet; when moving, the arms mimic the swaying branches of a tree.

AV

Marisol
American (b. Paris), b. 1930
The Family, 1969
Mixed media: wood, plastic, neon, glass
88" x 56" x 65" (223.5 cm x 142.2 cm x 165.1 cm)
Commissioned for Brooks Memorial Art Gallery through a grant from the
National Endowment for the Arts and matching funds from the Memphis Arts
Council, Brooks Fine Arts Foundation, and Brooks Art Gallery League 69.5

In 1967, Robert McKnight, the director of the Brooks, wrote to Marisol asking her
to create a Nativity for the museum. It was a logical request as Marisol was
internationally recognized for her figural groupings, as exemplified by the high-
profile commissions from *Time* magazine for portraits of Hugh Hefner and Bob
Hope. Born of Venezuelan parents in Paris, and raised in the United States and
Venezuela, she was well versed in the history of art as well as South American
popular culture. Originally envisioned as a complete Nativity, the project ended
with the three figures of the Holy Family.

Typical of Marisol's work, the figures are composed of both abstract and
representational elements and a variety of different media that combine here to
create a playful yet moving image of a traditional art historical subject. Mary and
Joseph are formed from block-like wooden boxes simply painted with flat color.
Mary's dress, covered with painted starbursts surrounded by collaged pieces of
glass, places her within the tradition of highly decorative and ecstatic Latin
American images of the Virgin. Both figures have cast plaster faces, hands, and
feet. Marisol, who repeatedly used self-portraits in her work to explore the roles
of women in society as well as her own identity, is the model for Mary. The Virgin's
holiness is conveyed through multiple means: she floats above the ground, has a
dazzling neon sun for a halo, is dressed in her traditional blue mantle, and has two
left hands bearing rings symbolizing her marriage to Joseph and God. Her womb
is a door that opens to expose a mirror in which all viewers can see themselves
reflected as a part of the Holy Family. The importance of Jesus, the smallest figure
in the scene, is signaled through the elaborate neon manger; the simplicity of his
unpainted body, almost completely carved of one piece of wood, stands out
against the rest of the brightly colored scene. Marisol blends materials associated
with advertising and commerce, such as neon and Astroturf, with fine art
conventions to produce a complex work that explores the role of women and
religion in contemporary society.

MP

Yousuf Karsh
Canadian (b. Armenia), 1908-2002
Muhammad Ali, 1970,* from the portfolio *Fifteen Portraits, 1983
Silver gelatin print
23 3/4" x 19 7/8" (60.3 cm x 50.5 cm)
Signed: lower left on mount
Gift of the David Walker Family in honor of Dr. Parks W. Walker 99.9.1

Born in Turkish Armenia, Yousuf Karsh took refuge in Syria at the age of fifteen, and subsequently immigrated to Canada in 1924. Later apprenticed to portrait photographer John Garo in Boston, Karsh learned the technical processes of photography and the effects of lighting. He was inspired, through the many encounters he had with influential and prominent individuals he met in Garo's studio, to create portraits of people who left their indelible mark on the world. Opening his own studio in 1931 in Ottawa, Karsh began to photograph significant 20th-century figures; notably, his portrait of Queen Elizabeth II appeared on Canada's one-dollar bill. The artist closed his studio in 1991, but not before documenting such important figures as Nelson Mandela and President Bill Clinton.

In all of his photographs, Karsh sought to capture the essence of the sitter by spending time with him or her before he made the photograph. Boxer Muhammad Ali was at a pivotal point in his career when he sat for this 1970 portrait. Ali was awarded the gold medal in boxing at the Rome Olympics in 1960. When he refused to be drafted for the Vietnam War in 1967, he was stripped of his heavyweight title, convicted of draft evasion, and sentenced to five years in prison. By 1970, with an appeal of his conviction still pending, he had been granted a boxing license in New York and was planning a comeback. That same year, at the age of twenty-eight, Ali sat for this portrait.

Rather than appearing in his boxing trunks and gloves, Ali chose to wear an elegant pinstriped suit to command the respect he felt he deserved. With his eyes assertively staring out at the viewer, he appears to issue a challenge. His shoulders are rolled forward defiantly and his broad fists are planted firmly on his hips, creating a boxy, angular composition. The boldly contrasting white cuffs and shirt collar, along with the pinstripes on his suit, direct attention to both his head and his hands, emphasizing the attributes that made him famous. Karsh's dramatic lighting also highlights Ali's forehead, underscoring the boxer's intellect, and contrasting it with his infamous physical prowess, which is only implied in this image.

KHD

Andy Warhol
American, 1928-1987
Electric Chair, 1971
Portfolio of ten silk screens, 232/270
10 each measuring 35 1/8" x 47 7/8" (89.2 cm x 121.4 cm)
Signed: verso
Memphis Brooks Museum of Art Purchase with funds provided
by the Jeniam Foundation, Michele and Arthur Fulmer, Kelly
and C.T. Fitzpatrick, an anonymous donor, Kaywin Feldman and
Jim Lutz, Rachel and Hank Gray, Neville and Warfield Williams,
Mary and Richard Scharff, David McCarthy and Marina Pacini,
Lee Pruitt, Monique and Charles Jalenak, and Margaret and
Pierce Ledbetter 2003.1a-i

Andy Warhol, generally considered the father of American Pop Art, produced his *Death and Disaster* screen paintings from 1962 to 1967. His canonical images in the series include car accidents, suicides, a mushroom cloud, civil rights riots, and Jackie Kennedy in Dallas (three examples of which are in the Brooks Collection). Among the most haunting of the series, however, are the electric chairs, which he completed as silk screens on both canvas and paper.

Critics disagree as to whether Warhol's art is noncommittal or political. Certainly capital punishment was one of the most hotly debated issues in the sixties. After his death, it was discovered that he collected images from World Wide Photo, a commercial photo archive.[1] Exactly when he bought the images remains unclear, but all of the electric chair paintings and prints are based on a photograph that is labeled on the back: "Sing Sing's Death Chamber. January 13, 1953." The text goes on to note that this is the chair in which Julius and Ethel Rosenberg will be executed. This information makes it difficult to view the electric chairs as anything but a condemnation of governmental power.

In 1971, Warhol produced a portfolio of ten screen prints on paper. Much of the original photograph is cropped so that the door with the ominous Silence sign over it does not appear. Nonetheless, the empty room with the chair, restraining straps dramatically visible, remains a disturbing image. Although the vacant chair grimly awaits its next occupant, the overall effect of the isolated chair, repeated in Warhol's signature palette of Pop colors, is also highly decorative. It is this dramatic contrast between engaging visual form and controversial subject matter that fuels the debates concerning his intentions.

MP

[1]Peter Halley, "Fifteen Little Electric Chairs," in *Andy Warhol Little Electric Chair Paintings* (New York: Stellan Holm Gallery, 2001), p. 41.

William Eggleston
American, b. 1939
Memphis, ca. 1971
Dye transfer print
12 1/16" x 17 1/4" (30.6 cm x 43.8 cm)
Eugenia Buxton Whitnel Funds 76.6.2

Memphis, the title of this photograph, is the birthplace and residence of William Eggleston, a leading figure in the evolution of color art photography. He attended Vanderbilt University, Nashville; Delta State College, Cleveland, Mississippi; and the University of Mississippi, Oxford. After his discovery, in 1962, of Henri Cartier-Bresson's book of photographs titled *The Decisive Moment*, he began to pursue photography seriously. Since 1966 he has worked almost exclusively in color, which was unusual at the time, as it was a commercial process and primarily used in advertising. Ten years later he was given a one-person exhibition at the Museum of Modern Art (MoMA) in New York, which provoked much controversy among critics, some of whom viewed his photographs as mere snapshots of random subjects.

Eggleston's departure from the traditional formality of black-and-white photography was intentional; his goal was to capture the real world by choosing to shoot seemingly unimportant places and people. His democratic way of seeing was influenced more by his personal vision than by previous artistic styles. Color, he believes, is a fundamental feature of perception, as well as a vital aspect of documenting daily life. Through his large-format prints of everyday subject matter, he creates iconic images of ordinary scenes.

One of his most famous works, *Memphis* was featured on the cover of *William Eggleston's Guide*, the exhibition catalogue for his 1976 show at MoMA. In a suburban neighborhood a tricycle sits on an expanse of concrete. Contrasted with the blue green of the tricycle are the grays of the sidewalk, the winter sky, the roofs of the houses, and the colorless grass. The tricycle is seen from an unusual perspective, making it appear gigantic. Dominating the foreground, it takes on a somewhat menacing presence as it dwarfs the homes and car in the background. Many of Eggleston's photographs, like this one, have vague titles or remain untitled. He prefers viewers to approach his photographs without preconceptions, forcing his audience to develop their own interpretations and conclusions. His works invite speculation and are layered with ambiguities.

KVG

William Christenberry
American, b. 1936
Cannon's Grocery, 1972
Chromogenic coupler print
3 1/4" x 4 7/8" (8.3 cm x 12.4 cm)
Anonymous gift in honor of Dr. Marcus Orr 89.13

William Christenberry
American, b. 1936
Cannon's Grocery, 1976
Wood, red soil, metal, Plexiglas, illustration board
(building): 10 3/4" x 27 1/2" x 16 1/2" (27.3 cm x 69.9 cm x 41.9 cm)
(base): 33" x 37 1/8" x 29" (83.8 cm x 94.3 cm x 73.7 cm)
Gift of Mr. and Mrs. Julien Hohenberg 89.4

William Christenberry is inextricably rooted to rural Alabama, a land of kudzu, red soil, farm buildings, churches, and roadside stores. Born in Tuscaloosa, he spent his childhood summers with his grandparents in nearby Hale County. He received his master's degree from the University of Alabama, taught at Memphis State University (today the University of Memphis), and currently teaches at the Corcoran School of Art in Washington, D.C. Although he works in many media, including painting, sculpture, installation, and photography, his subject matter is exclusively southern, reflecting the geography, architecture, and cultural history of his birthplace.

Pivotal in his career was his discovery, in 1959, of James Agee's *Let Us Now Praise Famous Men* (1941), which included Walker Evans' photographs of the Hale County of Christenberry's childhood. He began to reevaluate his own photographs, which at the time served merely as a reference for his paintings. After showing his work to Evans and receiving encouragement, Christenberry began to pursue photography seriously.

The artist first photographed Cannon's Grocery in 1972 and emphasized its rural locale by including a glimpse of the surrounding field and the unpaved road. The image is small but powerful, with the store's vibrant complementary colors echoed in the blue sky and clay-colored soil. The linear qualities of the building are repeated through the landscape—the horizontal bands of the grass, the dirt road, and the horizon. Christenberry also makes sculptures replicating the rural structures of his Alabama childhood; these miniature-scale models evoke a sense of nostalgia, bringing to mind boyhood toys and playthings. He realistically re-creates the appearance of the original building materials and old signs, and even incorporates actual objects from the site, such as the bed of Hale County dirt. Paying close attention to minute details, he reproduces the small tattered advertisements hanging in the windows, the weathered paint of the building's exterior, and the old door worn from use. Through his artwork, he immortalizes Cannon's Grocery, a country store and former hub of rural activity, as a cultural icon reminiscent of an earlier time.

KVG

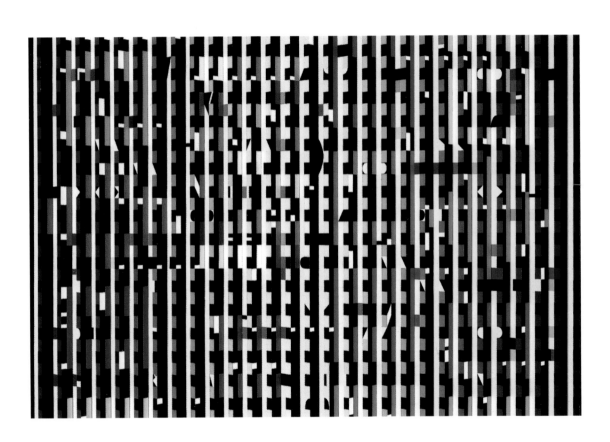

Yaacov Agam
Israeli, b. 1928
Lumière de Minuit, 1973
Oil on metal
32" x 49 5/8" x 2 3/4" (81.3 cm x 126 cm x 7 cm)
Gift of Mr. Irving Harris, Mr. and Mrs. Morrie A. Moss, Mr. and Mrs. Jack A. Belz, Mr. and Mrs. Ira A. Lipman, and Brooks Museum Purchase 83.17

Yaacov Agam, who was born the son of a rabbi in Rishon Le-Zion, Israel, was greatly influenced by his religious heritage and the doctrines of the Orthodox Judaic faith. He studied art at the Bezalel Academy of Arts and Design in Jerusalem from 1947 to 1948 and the Kunstgewerbeschule in Zurich in 1949. Agam was interested in the idea of life as dynamic rather than static, and adapted the concept into his art when he moved to Paris in 1951. He began to make kinetic art, which is sculpture that actually moves as a whole or in parts. At the same time, Agam also made art, such as *Lumière de Minuit*, that creates the optical illusion of movement as viewers change their position in relation to the object. The artist developed a special vocabulary to describe his work and calls this type of painting, which is intended to play with the complexities of human perception as the viewer moves from side to side, an "Agamomorph."

The picture plane is literally a three-dimensional surface with raised triangular columns onto which the artist has painted a grid of colorful geometric shapes in carefully placed repeating patterns. As the viewer moves from right to left, the image changes with every step. From the far right, one sees blocky white shapes and lines on a black background. Moving toward the center, the field changes to a reveal thick outlines of geometric shapes in vibrant pink, purple, yellow, orange, blue, green, and red. Continuing to the far left, one can see three alternating horizontal spectrums, in highly saturated color, with geometric shapes in black and white peppered throughout. Each of these views, and the many others achieved as the viewer changes position, presents a new and exciting perspective. What is normally a static picture is instead a lively image where metamorphosis is fundamental. The interaction between the viewer and the work of art creates a sense of discovery and magic, thus fulfilling the artist's desire for constant change and dynamism.

KHD

Romare Bearden
American, 1914-1988
In the Garden **from the portfolio** *The Prevalence of Ritual,* 1974
Silk screen in colors, 15/100
36" x 29" (91.4 cm x 73.7 cm)
Signed and dated: lower right
Gift of Art Today 75.5.1

Romare Bearden spent much of his adolescence in Harlem, New York, where he was introduced to, and strongly influenced by, the musical and cultural innovations of jazz. After graduating from New York University in 1935 with a degree in mathematics, he decided to become an artist, studying under George Grosz at the Art Students League and later at the Sorbonne in Paris. He was inspired by a wide array of influences, including Cubism, the Italian Renaissance, Social Realism, and classical Chinese landscape painting. Bearden worked in a variety of media, including collage, photomontage, painting, and printmaking.

His works are richly textured with visual metaphors from his past and from a range of literary, musical, and historical sources with themes paralleling those found in jazz, folk music, and urban and rural African American life. In *The Prevalence of Ritual*, a series of five serigraphs (the Brooks owns the complete series), Bearden depicts biblical and literary imagery that incorporates rituals, ceremonies, and myths. He often worked in the medium of collage, which is the technique of making compositions by gluing paper, fabrics, photographs, or other materials onto a flat surface. By combining abstract shapes and forms in bold colors and various overlapping patterns, Bearden achieved a collage-like effect through printmaking. The appearance of a lush, fertile oasis is created by filling the composition with abundant plant forms, brightly hued flowers, and exotic-looking birds—a metaphor for a modern-day Garden of Eden. The garden has long been a symbol for fertility and Eve, the first mother, is often depicted holding the forbidden fruit or in the act of plucking it. This contemporary Eve is African American and clothed in modern dress. She could personify the many roles of women through the ages: mothers gathering and providing food for their families, slaves and sharecroppers working in the fields, and women tending their flower and vegetable gardens. Bearden's image serves as a universal symbol bridging the gap between women of different times and places, and uniting them in their shared roles and rituals.

KVG

Sam Gilliam
American, b. 1933
Azure, 1977
Acrylic with collage on canvas
90" x 120" (228.6 cm x 304.8 cm)
Gift of Art Today 80.2

Sam Gilliam was raised in a large family, and in an effort to keep him busy, his mother introduced him to art at a young age. Although born in Mississippi, Gilliam spent his formative years in Louisville, Kentucky, where he received his BA and MA degrees in painting from the University of Louisville. Working in the style of Abstract Expressionism, Gilliam was influenced by Jackson Pollock's poured paintings and Helen Frankenthaler's and Morris Louis' stained canvases. Gilliam continues to reinterpret abstract painting through his use of saturated color, improvised materials, and unconventional application of paint.

Azure is exemplary of Gilliam's interest in and exploration of painterly depth and frontality. He often mixes acrylic paint with marble dust to produce a dense and tactile medium that, when applied, produces a surface similar to stucco. The painting is primarily black with pours and spills of peach and dark green. In the lower center, canvas strips are collaged onto the surface to achieve added texture and actual depth. The noticeably raised collage radiates from the most centralized rectangle, establishing a focal point. Unlike the dense ground, the strips are loosely stained, leaving the weave of the canvas visible. Gilliam's use of layered coats of color and collage draws attention to the means by which he creates his art.

AV

Nancy Graves
American, 1940-1995
Folium, 1978
Oil and encaustic on canvas
60" x 90" (152.4 cm x 228.6 cm)
Gift of Art Today, purchased with matching funds from the National Endowment for the Arts 79.3.1

From early in her career, Nancy Graves was intrigued with the direct connections between art and nature. Born in Pittsfield, Massachusetts, she grew up visiting the Berkshire Museum, where her father worked. The mixture of art and natural history collections the museum housed was a major influence on Graves, whose art encompasses natural history and paleontology. After receiving a degree in English from Vassar College, she was awarded a second undergraduate degree and an MFA degree from Yale University.

Her body of work is diverse, ranging from life-size polyurethane and burlap camels, large-scale bones made of wax, and drawings inspired by Paleolithic cave art and lunar maps, to a series of works based on camouflage, as well as energetic color displays. She abstracts natural phenomena, repeatedly challenging the viewer to examine art in relation to reality. Graves does not replicate nature, but investigates the ways physical objects are perceived and how they may be conceptualized.

Folium, the geological term for a thin stratum of metamorphic rock, parallels the many layers of Graves' artistic career embedded in this painting. Initially the images appear to be nonrepresentational, but on closer inspection, shapes, patterns, and references to the artist's past work emerge. The brown forms in the center represent a piece of her own sculpture made of bone formations; the positioning of the object anchors the composition, much like the piece itself served as a foundation for the artist's later work. She suggests additional bones through loosely connected black dashes and dots. The primary-hued circles and mauve and turquoise animal patterns recall her earlier *Camouflage* series, while the broad energetic swirls of color refer to the artist's study of Hurricane Camille. Through her use of shape, line, and color, Graves has created a vibrant multilayered design incorporating, in a single composition, many different stages of her work.

KVG

250

Elizabeth Murray
American, b. 1940
Tempest, 1979
Oil on canvas
120" x 170" (304.8 x 431.8 cm)
Gift of Art Today, purchased with matching funds from the National Endowment for the Arts 80.7

Elizabeth Murray's distinctively shaped canvases break the traditional boundaries of the two-dimensional picture plane. Her sculptural paintings playfully blur the line between the painting as an object and the painting as a space for depicting objects. Often her nonfigurative pieces suggest human characteristics, personalities, or emotions through an interaction of colors and shapes.

Inspired by Giorgione's *The Tempest* (1505), Murray was more interested in evoking a mood than depicting a clearly defined narrative. She, like the Italian Renaissance painter, created a feeling of unease by pairing disparate forms and colors. Through her use of complementary colors, she generates a sense of energy; the effect of the vibrant green on a red background and the orange over the blue is electrifying. Breaking through the rounded forms of orange and green, the yellow zigzag lines mimic lightning bolts while accentuating the sharp points of the canvas itself. The dynamic qualities of the storm are further emphasized through the juxtaposition of the large, round shapes with the angular forms in the composition and the multisided canvas. Through this dissonant union, the artist elicits palpable tension. Everything is electrified, in flux, and exploding.

Tempest represents an important turning point in the artist's career. It is one of her first "shaped" canvases, and one of her first paintings to be placed in a museum collection. Born in Chicago, Murray received her BFA degree from the Art Institute of Chicago and earned her MFA degree at Mills College in Oakland, California.

KVG

Robert Arneson
American, 1930-1992
Brick Self-Portrait, 1981
Ceramic
63 1/4 " x 17 1/4" x 18" (160.7 cm x 43.8 cm x 45.7 cm)
Signed and dated: left and right base
Gift of Art Today, Robert Fogelman, Dr. Tom Gettelfinger, Wil and Sally
Hergenrader, Carla Hubbard, Mickey Laukhuff, Marjorie Liebman, Jan Singer,
and Zeno Yeates 85.7

During his tenure at the University of California at Davis from 1962 until his death of
cancer in 1992, Robert Arneson developed one of the most important fine art
programs in the world devoted to ceramics. He was greatly influenced by the
Expressionist work of fellow Californian Peter Voulkos (also represented in the
Brooks Collection), who had studied Pablo Picasso's works in clay. Growing more
adventurous from this exposure, Arneson rejected the idea that ceramic art should
be only utilitarian or decorative, and began breaking previously established
sculptural boundaries by creating nonfunctional clay pieces. Along with his UC Davis
students, Arneson shaped a dynamic variation of Pop Art that came to be known as
Funk Art. Marked by a spontaneous, experimental treatment of clay, Funk
embodied an irreverent, earthy, and carefree style.

Throughout his career Arneson was a prolific producer of self-portraits, each one
seeming to reveal another dimension of his identity. *Brick Self-Portrait* is an
abstraction comprised of a column of ceramic bricks, each handcrafted and
stamped "Arneson," at once identifying the artist while using a brick mason's
branding technique to parody the more ornate maker's marks found on fine china.
At the top of the column several bricks balance precariously in a playful progression.
The highest brick is the most elaborate, depicting the artist's eyebrows, eyes, and
nose. Arneson's use of brick accents his desire to push clay beyond its traditional
ceramic limits, emphasizing rustic strength rather than delicate beauty.

One of America's most original sculptors, Arneson is often credited with reinventing
American figurative ceramics by integrating elements of sculpture and painting
within his large-scale, iconoclastic pieces. By fashioning visual puns regarding clay
as a fine art medium, Arneson challenged the hierarchies of East Coast art traditions
and allowed his followers greater freedom of expression. *Brick Self-Portrait*
exemplifies the attempt to constantly reinvent his practice and defy expectations of
what ceramics, and art in general, could do and become.

JW

James Surls
American, b. 1943
Me, the Dragon and the Sword, 1982
Live oak and maple
73" x 29 1/2" x 34" (185.4 cm x 74.9cm x 86.4 cm)
Gift of Art Today, purchased with matching funds from the National Endowment for the Arts 82.9

Sculptor James Surls lives in Splendora, Texas, where he creates sculpture from the wood grown on his thirty-acre farm. He received his BS degree from Sam Houston State College in Huntsville, Texas, in 1966, and his MFA degree from Cranbrook Academy of Art in Bloomfield Hills, Michigan, in 1969. After twelve years of teaching at the University of Houston, Surls decided in 1982 to devote himself to making art full-time. His complex sculptures frequently begin as succinct drawings that function as blueprints for the three-dimensional work he creates by cutting, chopping, peeling, carving, whittling, burning, scoring, and joining wood to produce his fantastic beings. His sculptures are often derived from his personal experiences, and the results can be interpreted as highly charged metaphors for the artist's personal feelings.

The aggressive sculpture *Me, the Dragon and the Sword* expresses an inner conflict.[1] A warrior, indicated by an arm brandishing a smoothly polished sword, does battle with the roughly carved dragon, who has been stabbed in the jaw by a second sword. Three wide eyes are incised on the top of the dragon's gnarled head, with their pupils burned into the wood. The outline of a hand has been carved into the back of the dragon's horn, and rubbed with lead to create a black line, a small but significant indication of the warrior contained within. The tumultuous struggle is balanced on three blackened legs that mimic the dragon's singular horn. It is left to the viewer to determine where one figure ends and the other begins. Surls also left it ambiguous as to who will win this swirling battle. Seeing himself as both warrior and dragon, he created this metaphorical struggle as a means of exploring his difficult decision to stop teaching. The artist's personal conflict is also a poetic allegory for survival in both the natural and the man-made world.

KHD

[1] James Surls, telephone conversation, July 9, 1982.

Michele De Lucchi
Italian, b. 1951
First, 1983
Plastic laminate, wood, enameled metal
35.4" x 27.2" x 19.7" (89.9 cm x 69.1 cm x 50 cm)
Memphis Brooks Museum of Art Purchase 86.33

Founded in Milan in 1981, MEMPHIS was a collaborative of international designers, architects, and artists. The name MEMPHIS originated from a Bob Dylan song titled "Stuck in Mobile with the Memphis Blues Again." The track repeatedly played in the studio and the designers felt that Memphis was the perfect identity for their own endeavors. The name suggested references to diverse cultural experiences such as the history of cotton production, American blues, rock and roll, and the ancient city of Memphis, Egypt. Although the group avoided formulating a manifesto, they presented an alternative to the tenets of International Modernism, which was known for its focus on function and simplicity of form. Departing from the functionality of Modernist design, MEMPHIS sought to bring a whimsical, surreal, and exciting quality to its projects.

Combining sources and materials that were both expensive and affordable, decorative and spare, MEMPHIS found inspiration in plastic laminated countertops, Art Deco, Hollywood, and early civilizations. Introducing color, shape, and pattern back into furniture, Michele De Lucchi's *First* chair explores the circle as a design element and humorously questions the effectiveness of the object. The chair is relatively small and appears more decorative than useful. A set of narrow metal legs supports the seat of the chair, while a thin rod curves up from the front legs to form the armrests and back. A dynamic interaction is created between the flat and rounded elements, from the bright turquoise vertical back, to the glossy black spheres, and back to the flat lacquered horizontal seat. De Lucchi's use of simple shapes and shiny colors establishes a spatial balance between two- and three-dimensionality, as well as a play between highly lacquered wood and matte industrial metal.

AV

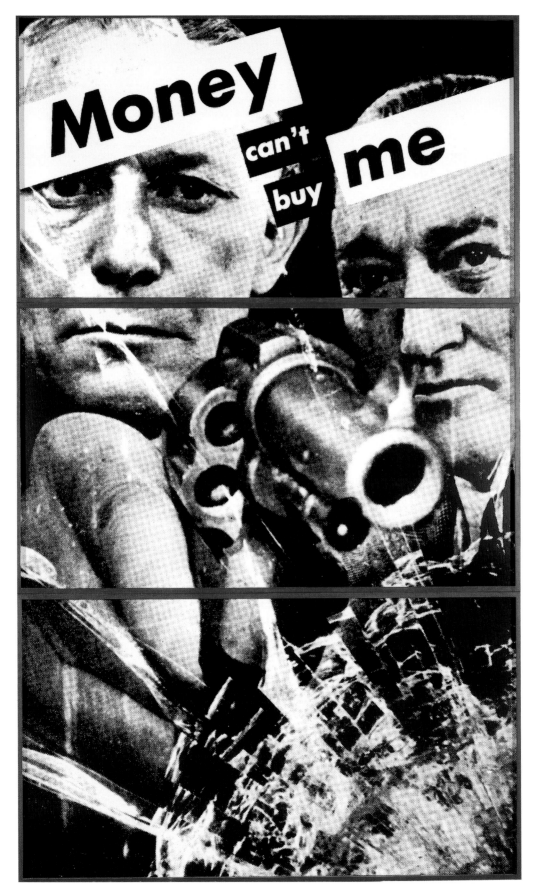

Barbara Kruger
American, b. 1945
(Untitled) Money can't buy me, 1984
Photolithograph with silk screen overlay
123 1/2" x 72 1/8" (313.7 cm x 183.2 cm)
Purchased by Art Today, Susan Austin, Eleanor Baer, Robert F. Fogelman, Allen
and Minna Glenn, Wil and Sally Hergenrader, Mickey Laukhuff, Bickie
McDonnell, Stella Menke, Jan Singer, Marie Thompson, Ruth Williams, and
Richard and Barbara Wilson 84.5.2a-c

Barbara Kruger's broadly political collages, prints, and installations question societal power structures through images culled from the mass media. An experienced graphic designer from her tenure at the fashion magazine *Mademoiselle*, Kruger utilizes her knowledge of advertising techniques to highlight her antiauthoritarian concerns. This is made apparent with her skill at "hailing," an important advertising method by which viewers are simultaneously beckoned and enraptured by the picture before them.[1] By scanning and selecting images, gauging their rhetorical potential, and then readjusting their dimensions into an iconic compositional order, Kruger concentrates visual impact into a cohesively focused whole that she refers to as "vernacular signage." Her manipulations of old newspaper, magazine, and movie poster images into probing photomontages follow a distinguished art historical tradition of socially conscious collages dating from the German Dadaists of the 1910s and 1920s, particularly those by Hannah Hoch and John Heartfield.

At a height of over ten feet, the vertical black-and-white triptych *Money can't buy me* looms over viewers with a confrontational energy reminiscent of early Soviet propaganda posters. Kruger believes paternalism and consumerism are detrimental to society, and boldly asserts an independence from these influences through the print's slogan. The stern countenance of founding FBI Director J. Edgar Hoover looks on as an equally dour companion seems to have just fired a giant revolver and shattered a pane of glass, delivering a visual punch that meets the viewer one-on-one. The men's scowls, the pistol, and the broken glass all symbolize repression and disdain for the kind of individual autonomy that Kruger embraces. Set into red frames dividing the picture plane into three sections, the image captivates with a fixating immediacy that leaves a lasting impression while provoking viewers to ponder their own relationships with authority.

JW

[1]Kate Linker, *Love for Sale: Words and Pictures of Barbara Kruger* (New York: Harry N. Abrams, Inc., 1990), pp. 14-17.

Michael Spano
American, b. 1949
Portrait of a Man, 1987
Silver gelatin print
35 5/8" x 26 3/4" (89.5 cm x 67.9 cm)
Signed: lower right
Memphis Brooks Museum of Art Purchase 89.6

A native of New York City, Michael Spano received his MFA degree from Yale University in 1978, and has since exploited his personal experiences of living in New York within his large-scale, black-and-white photographs. Spano creates surreal images that are both mysterious and evocative by capturing his city-dwelling subjects within a nebulous urban environment. The fantastic imagery is further enhanced through his use of solarization. First noticed in daguerreotypes of the 1840s, solarization is caused by extreme overexposure of the negative during the development process. The result is a reversal of tones leaving the whole or part of the negative image as a positive, causing the finished photograph to have a metallic quality. Influenced by Man Ray and his exploration of solarization during the 1920s, Spano captures ordinary human subjects yet transforms them through this photographic technique into remarkably expressive images.

Portrait of a Man depicts an aging man rendered in profile, looking out toward the street. He, like many of Spano's subjects, is solitary, emphasizing the isolation of modern urban life. With a pensive expression, the man looks away from the camera, not engaging with the viewer. His furrowed brow, the veins on his temple, the wrinkles and creases of his jowl, and his thinning white hair remain clearly delineated. The solarization process is particularly evident in the reversal of the tones of his coat, marked by the silvery gray highlights and the crisp black outline of the form. Spano further manipulates the image by solarizing the buildings and trees. The dream-like quality is heightened by the narrow plane of focus, with both the man's coat in the foreground and the structures behind him reduced to a blur. Were it not for the sharp focus of the man's head, it would almost appear that his entire form is melting into the background, reinforcing Spano's concept of urban isolationism.

KHD

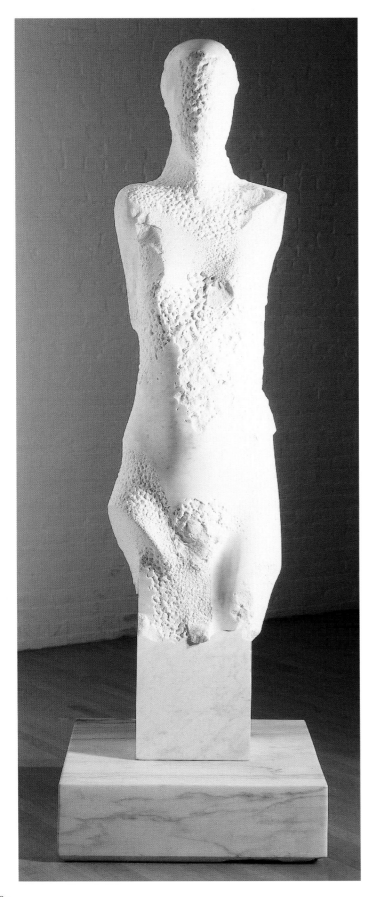

Manuel Neri
American, b. 1930
Carrara 88, 1988
Carrara marble
73 1/4" x 18" x 13" (186.1 cm x 45.7 cm x 33 cm)
Gift of Art Today, its Rosamund Bernier Fund, and the following: (Sustainers) Mrs. James D. Robinson, Charles Cowles Gallery, Wil and Sally Hergenrader, and Mickey and Ralph Lewis Laukhuff; (Donors) Dr. Thomas Gettelfinger, Dr. Rushton Patterson Jr., Richard and Barbara Wilson, and an anonymous donor; (Supporters) d'Arts, William and Jean Clouspy, Mr. and Mrs. Michael McDonnell, Hubert F. and Emily Fisher, Mr. and Mrs. Clyde C. Hudson, Mrs. Arline Krelstein, Joe and Jeannie Magdovitz, Dr. James D. Patterson, Mrs. Greenfield Polk, Mrs. N.S. Tommie Shobe, H. Ward Singer, Ann and Walker Uhlhorn, and Mr. and Mrs. Zeno L. Yeates 89.30

Born in northern California, Manuel Neri was first influenced by the experimental activities of jazz musicians and Beat poets working in San Francisco and the Funk aesthetic they shared. He soon became associated with the Bay Area artists, including painters Elmer Bischoff, David Park, and Richard Diebenkorn, in the 1950s and 1960s. Drawing from these experiences, and taking inspiration from the principles of Abstract Expressionism, Neri began exploring new materials and forms for figurative sculpture, coating his plaster humanoid works with bold, colorful brushstrokes. An astute artist aware of the properties of his materials and the scope of art historical precedents, Neri early on manifested aspects of the gouged, hand-modeled style of Auguste Rodin (see page 120) and Alberto Giacometti's abstracted figuration.

With *Carrara 88* Neri continues his examination of the human form through the medium of marble. Carrara marble is renowned as perhaps the finest in the world and was used most famously by Michelangelo for his monumental *David* (1501-1504). Visiting the Tuscan city in Italy's Appenine mountains, Neri enacted a sculptor's ritual very similar to that which artists centuries before him would have followed, from picking out the stone to shaping it with hammer and chisel. A lone female figure with truncated arms and legs seems to emerge as if from a fog. This effect echoes that of Michelangelo's *Dying Slave and Rebellious Slave* (ca. 1513), where the unfinished state of the figure evokes an expressive pathos that most probably would have been lost had the sculpture's surface been more fully completed. Neri demonstrates a refined awareness of texture by contrasting smoothly polished surfaces with areas of roughly pitted chisel marks. He has consciously positioned this work within an art historical trajectory bearing stylistic and symbolic affiliations with the master sculptors of the Italian Renaissance. By acknowledging his artistic predecessors in this manner, Neri simultaneously pays homage to their skill and insinuates himself into the company of their recognized genius, while making his own mark toward defining a distinctive variant upon the genre.

JW

John Buck
American, b. 1946
Full Circle, 1992
Jelutong wood, acrylic paint
81 5/8" x 32 1/2" x 16" (207.3 cm x 82.6 cm x 40.6 cm)
Gift of AutoZone, Inc. 2001.15.6

Printmaker and sculptor John Buck was born in Iowa and earned his BFA degree from the Kansas City Institute and School of Design. In 1972 he received his MFA degree from the University of California, Davis, where he studied with Robert Arneson (see page 252). His freestanding narrative sculptures are comprised of disconnected elements and figures that maintain a precarious equilibrium with each other. Flames, sticks, flowers, geometric shapes, and headless human figures are recurring images in both his sculpture and his prints.

Full Circle is characteristic of Buck's sculpture in the choice of universalizing themes and exotic material. The artist states that the title, *Full Circle*, refers to his interest in the folk art of diverse cultures, particularly the kachina dolls of the Pueblo people.[1] Given during ceremonies, kachina dolls are presented to girls and young women to teach them the importance of religion and familiarize them with the spirits known as the kachina. Jelutong wood is a soft lumber indigenous to Malaysia that is not strong enough to be used as a building material, but works well for sculpture. Although Buck leaves his carved marks visible, choosing not to smooth or sand the wood, he covers the surface with paint. Here, a headless figure carries an assemblage of symbolic objects on its shoulder: a circle with leaves and a human head appended; and a figurine of a headless woman who shares a neck with an inverted headless man. The only color in the work is found in the two delicate but vibrant red-orange flowers that surmount the paired branches chained together; their vertical orientation parallels the human form to the right. Drawing on natural forms and world religions, Buck posits the connectedness of all life.

AV

[1]John Buck, Email correspondence with author, June 15, 2004.

Carrie Mae Weems

American, b. 1953

From Here I Saw What Happened and I Cried, 1995-1996

C-prints with sandblasted text on glass

2 panels: 43 1/2" x 33 3/8" (110.5 cm x 84.8 cm)

8 panels: 26 3/4" x 22 3/4" (67.9 cm x 57.8 cm)

Purchased by Memphis Brooks Museum of Art with funds provided by the Morrie A. Moss Acquisition Fund, Kristi and Dean Jernigan, Storage USA, and Art Today; other funding from Kaywin Feldman and Jim Lutz, Rodney and Andrea Herenton, Elliot Perry, and Gayle Rose 2001.1.a-j

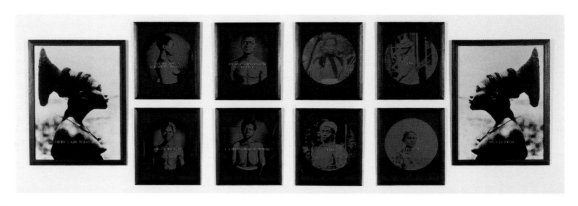

Carrie Mae Weems was commissioned by the J. Paul Getty Museum to respond to *Hidden Witness: African Americans in Early Photography*, an exhibition of mid-19th-century photographs. She rephotographed some of those images (along with late-20th-century photographs by Garry Winogrand [represented in the Brooks Collection] and Robert Mapplethorpe), enlarged them, printed them in saturated color, and covered the photographs with glass etched with text to create an installation of thirty-two components. The color, images, and text combine in *From Here I Saw What Happened and I Cried* to initiate an exploration of slavery and racial discrimination.

Her interest in politics appeared in Weems' work from the beginning—she began taking pictures of left-wing political events, including antiwar demonstrations and feminist marches, in the early 1970s. Adopting the documentary model of photographers such as Roy DeCarava, and appropriating both historical and contemporary imagery, she strives to effect social change through her art. Like her contemporaries Lorna Simpson and Barbara Kruger (see page 258), Weems works with series of images to give visual form to an idea. She further conceptualizes her artwork through the introduction of text, engaging the viewer in an actual discussion regarding the images presented.

That discussion begins here as the viewer reads the title, grapples with the identity of the "I," and questions what, exactly, has been seen. One position that can be taken is that of the African woman, who is appropriated from George Specht's 1927 photograph *Nobosodru, a Mangbetu Woman*, in the framing diptych. What she is witnessing in the central section—blood red images and charged text—produces an effect that is anything but neutral. Through the words on the final panel, the speaker emphatically empathizes with the victims of slavery and discrimination. Hence, for viewers, the process of determining who the "I" is—themselves, the artist, or the African woman—is central to the work.

MP

Donald Sultan
American, b. 1951
Black Egg and Tomatoes, August 4, 1998, 1998
Tar, Spackle, and oil on linoleum tile over Masonite
96" x 96" (243.8 cm x 243.8 cm)
Signed and dated: top left
Memphis Brooks Museum of Art Purchase; Morrie A. Moss Acquisition Funds
2000.6a-d

Still life painting is the representation of an arrangement of ordinary objects. This time-honored practice has captivated artists for centuries. Donald Sultan—who was born in Asheville, North Carolina, and received his BFA degree from the University of North Carolina, Chapel Hill, and his MFA degree from the School of the Art Institute of Chicago—continues to work within the genre. His depiction of objects draws attention to the visual qualities of form, color, texture, and composition. His bold, large-scale arrangements of eggs, dominoes, fruit, and buttons employ compositional methods and techniques that tie him to Modernist conventions.

Unlike traditional still life paintings where objects are realistically depicted on a table-like surface, Sultan reduces the objects to simple geometric forms presented from a bird's-eye perspective. With no indication of a plane on which objects rest, the painting is abstracted and flattened. Sultan often uses a Minimalist grid overlaid with an outsized everyday object as in *Black Egg and Tomatoes, August 4, 1998.* The painting begins with four conjoined four-foot-square Masonite boards, on top of which are affixed one-foot linoleum tiles that are then covered with tar. After drawing his image on the tar, Sultan carves into the surface and the holes he creates are filled with Spackle, sanded, and painted with oil. Areas that are left untouched, such as the large, elliptical egg, are all that remains of the original tar base. The process of extracting and then sealing areas of the painting creates a surface that is at once smooth yet physically dimensional. The egg appears to float over a black ground covered with small orange circular tomatoes. According to the artist, the black egg, found in Chinese culture, was a visually odd but nevertheless familiar and mundane object.[1] A solid void and a centralized weight, the egg anchors the composition.

AV

[1] Donald Sultan, telephone conversation with the author, June 25, 2004.

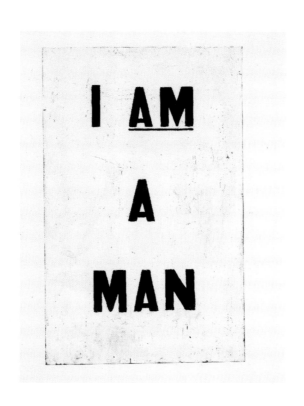

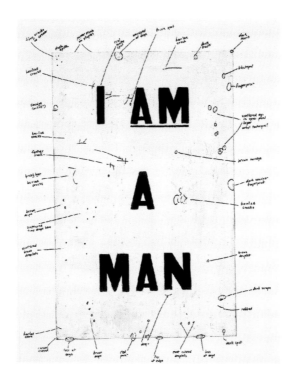

Glenn Ligon
American, b. 1960
Condition Report, 2000
Silk screen on IRIS prints
2 prints: 32" x 22 3/4" each (81.3 cm x 57.8 cm)
Signed: verso lower left
Memphis Brooks Museum of Art Purchase with funds provided by Blanchard and
Louise Tual, Paul and Phyllis Berz, and Jef and Babs Feibelman in honor of
Kaywin Feldman and Jim Lutz 2003-2a-b

Glenn Ligon's *Condition Report* is a diptych made from a direct photo scan of the
artist's 1988 painting *Untitled (I am a Man)*. Executed by a museum professional, a
condition report is a record of an artwork's physical condition, annotating both
accidental damage and natural deterioration. For this piece Ligon combines the
analytical appearance of the condition report with the technique of appropriation,
using a preexisting text to produce a new artwork in which the original meaning is
altered and expanded. Through this method he has established a structure from
which he can comment upon the current state of the civil rights movement, as well
as his own self-awareness as an African American gay man living in the wake of the
historical moment he references.

The phrase "I Am a Man" took on iconic status in Ernest Withers' (see page 214)
photographs of striking Memphis sanitation workers wearing placards emblazoned
with those words in 1968. An association with the subsequent assassination of Dr.
Martin Luther King Jr., who was in Memphis in support of the workers, has made the
phrase recognizable worldwide. It has come to symbolize the struggle of African
Americans to be treated with dignity and respect as equals in a time when such
equality was little more than a dream.

Ligon's work reveals his fascination with the influence of race, gender, sexuality, and
the power of language upon the formation of personal identity. By using this iconic
text of the civil rights movement, Ligon acknowledges the importance of the era
from which it derived, as well as the cultural resonance the phrase still possesses. He
also implies, through the subjection of his painting to the procedures of a condition
report, that the movement, like the painting, has weathered a great deal since its
origin. This print is also a self-portrait, the text placard covered with hand-drawn
observations of deficiencies that act as a surrogate for the artist's own image. Ligon
intertwines the personal and the political, asserting that despite criticism of his
condition he, like his protesting counterparts of 1968, deserves the dignity and
respect accorded to others.

JW

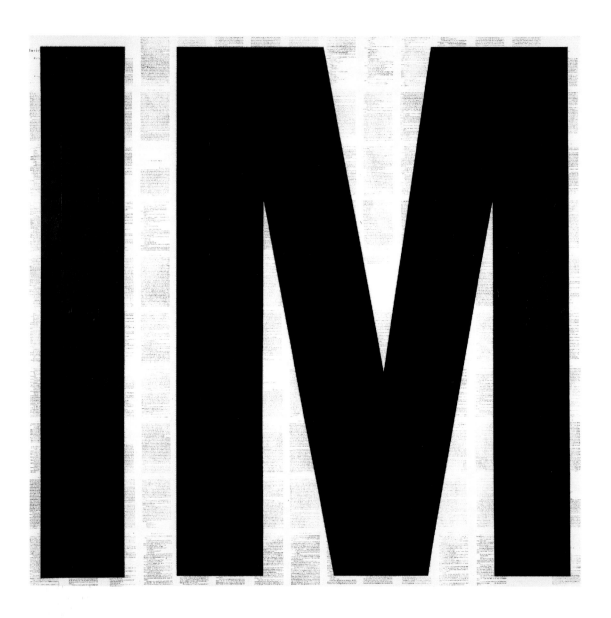

Tim Rollins and K.O.S. (Kids of Survival)
American, b. 1955
Invisible Man, 2001
Book pages, gesso, acrylic on canvas
74 1/4" x 72 1/4" (188.6 cm x 183.5 cm)
Signed and dated: verso left
Gift of the Deupree Family Foundation and the Turley Foundation 2001.3

As a member of Group Material, an artistic collaborative founded in 1980 that explored the relationships between politics and aesthetics, Tim Rollins demonstrated an interest in addressing social issues through art. In 1982 Rollins began teaching art in the Bronx and formed a collaborative called K.O.S. (Kids of Survival) with his students. Approaching art education in an interdisciplinary manner, Rollins and K.O.S. read a work of literature and then place the text in a larger historical and cultural framework. Through the connections and ideas that arise during the reading, Rollins and K.O.S. create a work of art that reflects their own interpretation of the work. The pages of the manuscripts are attached to the canvas, serving as both a literal and a conceptual ground. By the 1990s, Rollins had moved beyond the Bronx and had begun collaborating with schools across the country.

Based on Ralph Ellison's novel *Invisible Man*, which explores racial discrimination and feelings of isolation, the Brooks painting was created by Rollins and Memphis City Schools students from the Ida B. Wells Academy. The large bold letters—"I M"—that mark the pages of the book reference the title as well as the contraction of "I" and "am," which takes the form "I'm." This play on *Invisible Man* and "I'm" introduces a juxtaposition between being unnoticed (invisible) and having a presence (being). IM also alludes to the 1968 Memphis sanitation workers' strike that was documented by photographer Ernest Withers (see page 214). The sanitation workers wore plaques that read "I AM A MAN" as they picketed for fair working conditions. The assertive IM in the painting is inspired by and evokes the powerful lettering on the demonstration plaques. Although the strike was ultimately resolved favorably for the workers, it was tragically marred by the death of Dr. Martin Luther King Jr., who had come to Memphis to support the movement. *Invisible Man* symbolizes the strength of the human voice and its power to bring recognition and acknowledgment to everyone.

AV

274

Red Grooms
American, b. 1937
Tennessee S Curve, 2001
Enamel on epoxy on Styrofoam
46 1/2" x 36 5/8" (188.6 cm x 183.5 cm)
Signed: bottom center; dated: right edge
Memphis Brooks Museum of Art Purchase, Morrie A. Moss Acquisition Funds
2001.10

A painter turned sculptor, Charles Rogers "Red" Grooms was born and raised in Nashville, Tennessee. He studied at the Art Institute of Chicago; the New School for Social Research, New York; and the Hans Hoffman School in Provincetown, Massachusetts. Grooms is best known for his extravagantly scaled "sculpto-pictoramas," which are highly theatrical, three-dimensional installations that allow the viewer to walk through and interact with an environment completely created by the artist. He is also a prolific painter, printmaker, sculptor, performance artist, and filmmaker. Often combining elements from fine art and mass culture, Grooms treats his subjects with wit and satire, depicting them in an animated, cartoon-like manner, while incorporating exaggerated perspectives and vibrant colors.

In *Tennessee S Curve*, a combination painting and sculpture, or "stick-out" as Grooms calls these works because they jut out from the wall, he fashions a playful caricature of a Tennessee country road. Carved out of Styrofoam and coated with enamel and epoxy, the undulating surface of the relief sculpture extends the boundaries of the conventional picture plane. He pays homage to his home state with a brightly painted mountain highway complete with a rushing river, pine trees, wildflowers, a slithering snake, and a log truck. The curving road, which moves the viewer through the image, creates a sense of chaos in the sinuous bends of winding asphalt, the haphazard placement of vehicles, and the pattern of skid marks. Grooms humorously captures the typical country man in his pickup truck plastered with bumper stickers, a toolbox and a hunting dog in the back, raising his finger in a friendly gesture to each passerby. The natural beauty of the mountains is juxtaposed with the crudely made signs dotting the roadside: "See Rock City," "Thrills for the Whole Family at Lake Sequatchie," "Prepare to Meet the Lord," and "Ole' Time Tent Revival." With his unique mixture of materials, his unusual composition, and his sense of humor, the artist encapsulates the essence of the rural roads of eastern Tennessee.

KVG

Nam June Paik
South Korean, b. 1932
Vide-O-belisk, 2002
Vintage television cabinets, neon elements, and video
232" x 82 1/2" x 84 1/2" (589.3 cm x 209.6 cm x 214.6 cm)
Signed and dated: lower level
Commissioned by the Memphis Brooks Museum of Art; funds provided by the
Morrie A. Moss Acquisition Fund, the Hohenberg Foundation, Wil and Sally
Hergenrader, and the Bodine Company 2002.4

Through a range of installations, videos, global television productions, films, and
performances, Nam June Paik, widely considered the father of video art, has shaped
perceptions of the moving image in contemporary art. Paik, an instrumental figure
of the Fluxus movement, was influenced by the writings of John Cage, whose
theories of chance encouraged experimental work in art, music, and performance in
the 1950s and 1960s. By using the television and the portable camera—two devices
that were intended for mass communication and information distribution—for his
personal expression, Paik premiered an entirely new artistic medium and
revolutionized art making in the later half of the 20th century. He refers to museums
as modern versions of ancient temples that house society's cultural artifacts. When
Paik was commissioned by the Brooks for a site-specific installation, he accordingly
created a symbolic obelisk for the museum, a modern-day temple, that also
references the ancient Egyptian city of Memphis.

Vide-O-belisk exhibits Paik's interest in technology, communication, and music. The
sculpture is a nineteen-foot tower of vintage 1950s television cabinets, adorned with
neon signs symbolizing communication tools from ancient hieroglyphs to modern-
day apparatuses such as the telephone. The vivid magenta, blue, light blue, green,
yellow, and red bands of color that create the backdrop in each video form the
principal television color spectrum. Each cabinet plays one of three videos that are
continuously looped: one shows early moments in television history contrasted with
the essential mechanical parts of television technology; another superimposes
images of the museum's collection with images of ancient Egypt; and, finally,
keyboards and metronomes share the screen with images of Paik's early career with
his longtime collaborator, Charlotte Moorman; Cage; and the Fluxus movement.
Vide-O-belisk is a monument to the exchange of ideas and information through
various historical modes of communication and art.

AV

Index